STEP UP 1

Listening, Speaking, and Critical Thinking

Online Study Center

Additional information and activities for students can be found at the Online Study Center.

http://college.hmco.com/pic /teskeone1e

Online Teaching Center

Assessment and instructional materials for teachers can be found at the Online Teaching Center.

http://college.hmco.com/pic /teskeone1e

Margaret Teske
Mt. San Antonio College

Peggy Marcy
Mt. San Antonio College

W9-APH-340

Houghton Mifflin Company
Boston   New York

Publisher: Patricia A. Coryell
Editor in Chief: Suzanne Phelps Weir
Sponsoring Editor: Joann Kozyrev
Senior Development Editor: Kathy Sands Boehmer
Development Editor: Peggy Kehe
Editorial Assistant: Evangeline Bermas
Associate Project Editor: Eric Moore
Composition Buyer: Chuck Dutton
Associate Manufacturing Buyer: Brian Pieragostini
Executive Marketing Manager: Annamarie Rice
Marketing Associate: Andrew Whitacre

Cover image: © Boris Lyubner/Illustration Works

Printed in the U.S.A.

Library of Congress Control Number: 2006922140

Instructor's examination copy
  ISBN-10: 0-618-73205-5
  ISBN-13: 978-0-618-73205-0
For orders, use student text ISBNs
  ISBN-10: 0-618-35305-4
  ISBN-13: 978-0-618-35305-7

123456789-EB-10 09 08 07 06

CONTENTS

INTRODUCTION

Regarding Bloom's Taxonomy

Step Up 1 and 2: Listening, Speaking, and Critical Thinking, a two-level oral communication series, has effectively adapted Bloom's Taxonomy for the ESL classroom. Bloom developed his taxonomy in the 1960s as a logical sequencing pattern for the progression of learning. It begins with knowledge. At this stage, students start learning new information, such as new vocabulary and concepts. As they begin to grasp this new knowledge, they demonstrate their comprehension by doing activities that involve identifying, matching, and filling in missing information.

After demonstrating their comprehension, students experience working with their newly acquired knowledge through application. To apply it, they do a variety of tasks that challenge them to select and distinguish among a number of choices. At this stage, the contexts to which this new knowledge pertains are expanded upon, allowing students the opportunity to apply it in more widely varied situations.

After application, students "step up" to yet a higher order of thinking by carrying out activities that challenge them to analyze. This process of analysis helps students further internalize the varied aspects of what they have been studying.

At this point, students are prepared to take full ownership of their new knowledge via synthesis, a step that elevates learning to an experiential level.

As a culmination to Bloom's entire process, evaluation is the final step. At the end of each chapter, students evaluate their current level of mastery with regard to the chapter goals. Unit assessments available on the Online Teaching Center at http://college.hmco.com/pic/teskeone1e also help to determine each individual's level of achievement.

Text Organization

Step Up 1 is designed for low-intermediate learners of English as a Second Language. Each theme-based unit contains three chapters, a project, and online assessments, one for instructors to administer to students and one for students to use for self-assessment purposes. Each chapter begins with a self-reflection and a set of warm-up discussion questions. Pre-listening exercises introduce new vocabulary. The listening passages within a unit are based on a mini-lecture, a conversation, or a problem-solving situation. Speaking strategies are also introduced and practiced. Near the end of each chapter, "Stepping It Up" assignments challenge students to apply the strategies and vocabulary that have been the focus of that chapter and unit. A brief student self-evaluation follows that. At the end of each unit, there is a project designed to synthesize the content of the entire unit. The online assessments complete each unit and provide students with quantifiable feedback on their progress.

Components of Each Unit

Unit Skills

At the start of each unit, a list of skills introduces the focus of that unit.

Step One: Pre-Listening

In this initial pre-listening step, students work with a variety of vocabulary expressions; these will be used in the listening exercises and other activities that follow.

Step Two: Mini-Lecture/Conversation/Problem Solving

In Step Two of the *first* chapter of each unit, a mini-lecture serves as the content for the listening passage. Working with this type of content helps prepare students for listening to class lectures in other courses. As students progress through the text, the mini-lectures become longer and more challenging.

In the *second* chapter of each unit, Step Two supplies students with the chance to listen to everyday conversations. Working with this type of content can help bolster students' self-confidence and lay the groundwork for the types of social interaction it is hoped that students will pursue and engage in outside of class.

The content of the listening passage and other interactive activities in Step Two of the *third* chapter in each unit creates situations for students to work as a team to discuss and solve problems.

Step Three: Speaking

Step Three introduces strategies for speaking; these are related to the theme of a unit. Students interact in a variety of situations in order to practice and apply them. This is a good place for students to work on skills that will help improve scores on the speaking portion of the TOEFL® test.

Step Four: Stepping It Up Assignments

The assignments in Step Four give students practice in synthesizing all that they have learned. To what is usually a beyond-the-classroom experience, students apply what has been the focus of their work up to this point. This might involve, for example, interacting with others doing research or watching television. These assignments further support the development of fluency and self-confidence.

Unit Project

Ongoing preparation for each unit project is blended into most of the chapters themselves. These projects vary from unit to unit but are designed as a whole to challenge students to use their new expressions and strategies, to seek out relevant information, and to engage in an open exchange of information and viewpoints with classmates and others.

 ### Audio Program

Instructors should play the audio material in class. Students are encouraged to use the same audio program for out-of-class practice. Look for the listening icon throughout the book.

Additional recorded material for chapter and unit assessments is available to instructors.

⚛ *Online Study Center*   **Student Activities Online**

Students can easily access vocabulary flash cards (Prepare For Class), web activities (Improve Your Grade), and interactive chapter self-quizzes (ACE the Test!) at the Online Study Center. These can be useful for homework assignments or student self-enrichment. Look for the Online Study Center icon at key places within each chapter and direct students to http://college.hmco.com/pic/teskeone1e.

⚛ *Online Teaching Center*   **Teacher Resources Online**

To assist with using this textbook, several materials are available at the Online Teaching Center: teacher notes, answer key, audio script, handouts, transparencies, sample syllabus, chapter quizzes, and unit assessments.

Chapter and unit assessments can be printed and administered in class using the instructor audio. These tests evaluate students' ability to apply new vocabulary in sentence-level contexts, to understand listening passages, and to carry out speaking assignments.

For further reference, links to information about Bloom's Taxonomy are also provided.

TO THE STUDENT

You have many challenges ahead of you in college and university. The first one is to understand your classes. The second is to speak with your classmates, your instructors, and others on campus. *Step Up 1* prepares you to understand about everyday life in a variety of contexts. It does this first by introducing useful vocabulary and then by giving you opportunities to listen to and discuss content about real-life situations.

In each chapter, you learn new skills; then you have the chance to apply those skills. You will also evaluate your own progress. As you study each chapter, you will do a variety of listening and speaking exercises. Also, you will use your new skills when you work with other students to complete a unit project. Some of the skills that you learn help you to improve your score on the speaking portion of the TOEFL® test. Other skills will increase your self-confidence so that you can more comfortably join conversations with other people. Finally, you can take the interactive chapter self-quizzes at the Online Study Center to see how much you are improving.

ACKNOWLEDGMENTS

This book and its companion text, *Step Up 2*, have been a challenge and ultimately a joy to create as coauthors. We spent many months putting our ideas on paper and working out the format. These books have evolved with a lot of hard work and encouragement, especially from our colleagues at Mt. San Antonio College, Walnut, CA, who were so helpful with their assistance, ideas, and feedback.

We offer a special note of appreciation to the entire ESL publishing team at Houghton Mifflin, especially Kathy Sands Boehmer, Joann Kozyrev, and Susan Maguire. Susan encouraged us to become authors. Joann has been a source of support. Kathy has been incredibly patient and yet pushed us when we needed it. Furthermore, we greatly appreciate our development editor, Peggy Kehe, for her undying questions, comments, and e-mails. She truly made a positive difference in our manuscripts.

We would also like to thank the following reviewers who offered feedback and suggestions that shaped our revisions: Darenda Borgers, Broward Community College; Brent Green, Brigham Young University, Hawaii; Peggy and David Kehe, Whatcom Community College; Alba Pezzarossi, Wilbur Wright College; Margaret Redus, Richland College; Richard Christian Rice, Houston Community College; Denise Selleck, City College of San Francisco; Catherine Solange, Victor Valley College; Shirley Terrell, Collin County Community College; Julie Un, Massasoit Community College; Reina Welch, Miami Dade College; and Jeanne White, Gainesville College.

Margaret Teske
Peggy Marcy

UNIT I

SMALL TALK

Content Area:
Sociology

Skills You Will Learn

In this unit, you will:

Identify main points in a mini-lecture.

Ask questions of strangers.

Keep a conversation going.

Focus your listening on specific information.

Create expectations before listening.

Identify appropriate and inappropriate comments and situations.

Listen to confirm your expectation.

Compliment others.

State a need.

Request help.

Online Study Center

http://college.hmco.com/pic/teskeone1e

1

MAKING NEW FRIENDS on CAMPUS

Listening Focus: Mini-Lecture

Ask Yourself
How often do you make new friends?

STEP I: Pre-Listening

K N O W L E D G E

EXERCISE I: Discuss Warm-Up Questions

Discuss with a small group. Write some of your answers and share them with your class.

1. Do you talk with strangers? When? Why? Where, for example, in the bank, at the supermarket, or at the pharmacy?

2. In the United States, people in a group are uncomfortable with silence. Is this true in another country you are familiar with?

3. In what places or situations are you quiet in a group?

4. In what places or situations are you *not* quiet in a group?

5. Do you think it is easy to talk in a group of strangers? Is it easy in your native language? How about in English? Why or why not?

Online Study Center   **Prepare for Class**

EXERCISE 2: Preview Vocabulary

Match the expressions to their meanings.

_____	**1.** to converse	**a.** a curiosity
_____	**2.** a conversation	**b.** That is expensive.
_____	**3.** to cost	**c.** a fearful event
_____	**4.** That is a lot.	**d.** a similar opinion or thought
_____	**5.** frightening	**e.** to have as a price
_____	**6.** a situation	**f.** to talk about thoughts or ideas
_____	**7.** a frightening situation	**g.** shared; similar
_____	**8.** an agreement	**h.** to start talking
_____	**9.** an interest	**i.** a talk; a spoken exchange of ideas
_____	**10.** to break the silence	**j.** scary
_____	**11.** common	**k.** an event or condition

Guess the Idiom

Mr. Smith "hit the nail on the head."

    a. He was absolutely correct.

    b. He was strong and stubborn.

    c. He was crazy and wild.

EXERCISE 3: Fill in the Vocabulary

Use these words to fill in the blanks: *converse, interest, break, agreement, frightening, common.*

To _____ with strangers is _____ sometimes. If they _____ the silence first, then it is easy to show _____ in what they are saying. If I make an effort to be friendly, I usually find that we have some _____ interests. Then, I try to add an _____ to the conversation.

STEP 2: **Listening**

C O M P R E H E N S I O N

LISTENING STRATEGY

Listen for Main Ideas in a Lecture

Lectures usually begin with a short introduction to the topic and main ideas. Listen for the answer to these five questions:

Who? What? Where? When? How?

These questions help you focus on the main ideas.

Mini-lectures can make us nervous. We think that we must understand and remember everything! Do you read a newspaper in your native language? Do you ever watch the news on TV? If you do, you know that you don't remember everything, so, don't worry too much.

EXERCISE 4: **Identify Main Ideas in a Mini-Lecture**

A. Listen to "Mini-Lecture: Small Talk on Campus."

B. Listen again and write answers to these "main idea" questions.

1. What is a key to meeting and making new friends? Where can we meet new people?

2. How can we feel less nervous in a group situation when no one is talking?

3. What do you say before you ask a question?

4. When talking with a classmate for the first time, what is a possible question to ask?

5. How can you continue the conversation after your classmate answers your question?

C. Share your answers with your class.

EXERCISE 5: Ask Questions of Strangers

For each personal comment on the left, match the best question to add to it on the right.

_____	**1.** At a coffee shop, "I like to drink espresso coffee the best."	**a.**	Do I need a customs form?
_____	**2.** At the bookstore, "I have to buy $300 of books."	**b.**	How about your books?
_____	**3.** At an airport, "My plane leaves at 4 pm."	**c.**	What do you like (to drink)?
_____	**4.** At the post office, "I have to mail this overseas."	**d.**	What features do these have?
_____	**5.** At the bank, "I lost my ATM card."	**e.**	Did you find anything cheap?
_____	**6.** At a tea shop, "I saw (name of a movie) last week."	**f.**	How can I get a new card?
_____	**7.** At a store, "I found lots of bargains at this sale."	**g.**	Where are the cookbooks?
_____	**8.** At a movie rental, "I want to watch something funny."	**h.**	Do you have any suggestions?
_____	**9.** At the library, "I need information about French food."	**i.**	Have you seen that movie?
_____**10.**	At a cell phone store, "I'm thinking about a new phone."	**j.**	What time does your plane leave?

STEP 3: Speaking

APPLICATION

CULTURAL POINT

Ask Questions of Strangers

You may make a new friend whenever you talk to a stranger. In the United States, we ask semi-personal questions of strangers. However, we do not ask personal questions about marriage, age, weight, or religion. These are too personal.

Asking impersonal questions about the weather doesn't show much interest in that person. Asking about the weather is common. You need to ask more than questions about the weather in order to make a friend.

There is a balance between questions that are impersonal and questions that are too personal. Semi-personal questions are the best.

- **Too Personal:** Are you married? How old are you? How much money do you make? How much do you weigh? We can ask these questions if we have a close relationship with someone.

- **Semi-Personal:** Have you seen any good movies lately? What do you think of that basketball team? How was your vacation? Do you have a job? What's your next class? Do you want to join our study group? (These are the best.)

- **Not Personal Enough:** It's really raining hard, isn't it? Have you seen the snow? What time is it? (These are too common to show personal interest.)

EXERCISE 6: Write Questions to Ask Strangers

A. Write some examples of semi-personal questions to ask strangers in English.

1. In a supermarket: _____

_____?

2. At a bookstore: _____

_____?

3. In class before the teacher arrives: _____

_____?

B. Talk with your class about examples of good semi-personal questions. Share your ideas.

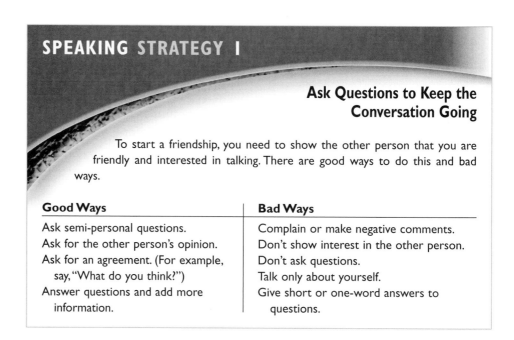

SPEAKING STRATEGY 1

Ask Questions to Keep the Conversation Going

To start a friendship, you need to show the other person that you are friendly and interested in talking. There are good ways to do this and bad ways.

Good Ways	Bad Ways
Ask semi-personal questions.	Complain or make negative comments.
Ask for the other person's opinion.	Don't show interest in the other person.
Ask for an agreement. (For example, say, "What do you think?")	Don't ask questions.
	Talk only about yourself.
Answer questions and add more information.	Give short or one-word answers to questions.

 ## EXERCISE 7: Evaluate the Conversations

Decide whether each conversation on the recording includes a good way or bad way to help people to continue talking. Discuss why. (Hint: Four of them are "bad.")

	Good Ways	Bad Ways
1.	_____	_____
2.	_____	_____
3.	_____	_____
4.	_____	_____
5.	_____	_____
6.	_____	_____
7.	_____	_____
8.	_____	_____

🎧 EXERCISE 8: Keep the Conversations Going

Listen to the recording. Add agreement or questions to continue the conversations.

SITUATION: The first day of math class at Sunterra College

Example 1

Person A:	Hey, have you been to the lab yet?
Person B:	No, I haven't. I need a lab partner. Do you have one?
Person A:	<u>Not yet. Do you want to be my partner?</u>

Example 2

Person A:	Have you ever had a class with this professor before?
Person B:	Yeah, and he's pretty hard. He gives lots of homework.
Person A:	<u>I guess we'll be busy then.</u>
Person A:	<u>Do you want to study together after class sometime?</u>

Conversation 1

Person A:	Hey, is that the book for this class?
Person B:	Yeah, it's really heavy and big. I think we'll have to work very hard, don't you think?
Person A:	_____

Conversation 2

Person A:	Do you know anything about this professor?
Person B:	I heard that he was pretty easy.
Person A:	_____

Conversation 3

Person A:	Haven't I seen you at the Valley View Apartments? Do you live there?
Person B:	Yeah. I'm new to the college. Do you live there, too?
Person A:	_____
Person B:	_____

Conversation 4

Person A:	Hi, haven't I seen you in another class today?
Person B:	_____
Person A:	_____

Conversation 5

Person A:	What's the name of the book for this class?
Person B:	_____
Person A:	_____

SPEAKING STRATEGY 2

Add Agreement to Keep the Conversation Going

Another way to keep the conversation going is to respond with agreement. This shows people that you want to keep talking. Here are some short expressions to show that you agree.

I know (what you mean).
I can see that.
I agree with you (there).
Exactly!
That's really true.

I guess so.
I'm afraid you're right.
Yeah, I heard the same thing.
I hope you're right.
You hit the nail on the head.

EXERCISE 9: Practice Speaking for TOEFL® Success

Give a 1-minute talk about how you can keep a conversation going when you meet a stranger. Here are some questions to guide you:

Where can you talk with strangers?

What expressions are appropriate to say to keep the conversation going?

What can you say to show agreement? Give a specific example.

What kinds of questions stop the conversation?

STEP 4: Stepping It Up

EXERCISE 10: Do Fast Introductions

A. Ask the three questions in the chart of as many students as possible in 15 minutes. Ask, listen, and add an agreement when possible. Fill in the chart as you go, or make a longer chart on a separate piece of paper. Here is an example introduction with Margaret:

Person A:	What's your name?
Person B:	Margaret. What is yours?
Person A:	I'm Kerry. Where are you from?
Person B:	I'm from Thailand.
Person A:	Oh yeah? I like Thai food. (Agreement) How do you come to class?
Person B:	By bus, it takes a long time.
Person A:	I know what you mean. (Agreement)

	What is your name?	Where are you from?	How do you come to class?	Write your own semi-personal question here.
1	Margaret	Thailand	By bus. It takes a long time.	
2				
3				
4				
5				

B. As a class, make a chart of everyone's semi-personal questions. Post the chart on the classroom wall (if possible) for future use.

EVALUATION

EXERCISE 11: Evaluate Your Learning

A. Check (√) all of the items that you have learned in this chapter.

- ☐ How to identify main ideas in a mini-lecture.
- ☐ How to ask questions of strangers.
- ☐ How to respond with agreement.
- ☐ How to keep a conversation going.

B. Choose one of the items you checked. Write at least three sentences about what you learned.

_____

_____

_____

_____

_____

_____

_____

_____

_____

_____

Online Study Center   **ACE the Test!**

TROUBLING CONVERSATIONS

Listening Focus: Conversation

Ask *Yourself*
How do you react to troubling conversations?

STEP 1: Pre-Listening

K
N
O
W
L
E
D
G
E

EXERCISE 1: Discuss Warm-Up Questions

Discuss with a small group. Write some of your answers and share them with your class.

1. Do you usually work by yourself or with a friend?
2. Do you do a better job at your homework when you study with a friend or by yourself? Why?
3. In your opinion, is it okay for males and females to study together? Why or why not?
4. In what situations do you feel shy?
5. How do you react when you have a conversation that upsets you?

Online Study Center   **Prepare for Class**

EXERCISE 2: Preview Vocabulary 1

Match the expressions to their meanings.

_____ 1. pretty tough   a. lots of/a lot of

_____ 2. tutoring   b. not busy

_____ 3. available   c. difficult

_____ 4. folks   d. teaching one-to-one

_____ 5. loads of   e. parents

EXERCISE 3: Preview Vocabulary 2

Match the idioms to their meanings.

_____ 1. tough it out   a. understand it/fix it

_____ 2. tough luck   b. do something that is difficult

_____ 3. out of town   c. do something different from usual (usually a bad thing)

_____ 4. figure it out   d. bad luck

_____ 5. act up   e. away from home

STEP 2: Listening

COMPREHENSION

LISTENING STRATEGY

Focus Your Listening

Good listening starts before you begin talking in a conversation. If possible, listen first. Then, find out the situation. Learn who is talking. This is like building mailboxes in your brain. Identify missing information that you need to know before you begin talking. Use the same questions (such as "Who?" or "What?") that you practiced in the Listening Strategy box in Chapter 1. Then, as you listen, you can put the information in the correct mailbox. If you prepare before talking, you will ask good questions and make good comments.

1. **Listen first** and find out the situation.
2. **Learn** who is talking.
3. **Identify missing information** that you need to know. For example, if you want to know who, listen for a name. If you want to know why, listen for a reason. If you want to know where, listen for a place.
4. **Focus** your listening on that specific information.

EXERCISE 4: Create Expectations 1

A. Before you listen to "Conversation 1: A Study Plan," write the WH question words in the blanks. (Hint: who = a name; where = a place; what = a thing; why = a reason; when = a time)

1. ___Who___ are the two people talking? *(Listen for names.)*
2. __________ does Pam need help with? *(Listen for a thing.)*
3. __________ does Mike offer to help her? *(Listen for a reason.)*
4. __________ will they meet? *(Listen for a time.)*
5. __________ will they meet? *(Listen for a place.)*

B. Listen to Conversation 1 and write your answers below to the questions in Part A. Check your answers with a partner.

1. ______________________________
2. ______________________________
3. ______________________________
4. ______________________________
5. ______________________________

EXERCISE 5: Discuss Your Expectations 1

 A. Listen again to Conversation 1 and answer the questions with a partner.

1. Why is Mike going to help Pam?

2. Where are they going to meet to work on homework?

3. When are they meeting?

4. Will there be some trouble? What do you think will happen?

B. Rewrite the end of the conversation so that they avoid possible trouble. Write on a separate piece of paper.

Pam: _Maybe you could come to my house and help me with my homework?_ _____

Mike: _____

Pam: _____

EXERCISE 6: Create Expectations 2

A. Before you listen to "Conversation 2: A Problem with a Computer," write the kind of information to listen for in each question. Write *place, thing, reason, response,* or *time* in each blank.

1. Where are Angela and Harry? (*Listen for a* _____.)

2. What is Angela's major in college? (*Listen for a* _____.)

3. Why does Harry feel lucky? (*Listen for a* _____.)

4. What has been acting up? (*Listen for a* _____.)

5. Why does Harry want Angela's phone number?

(Listen for a _____ *.)*

6. How does Angela answer about her phone number?

(Listen for a _____ *.)*

7. When can Harry call Angela? *(Listen for a* _____ *.)*

8. Why does Harry end the conversation? *(Listen for a* _____ *.)*

B. Listen to the recording for Conversation 2 and write your answers below to the questions in Part A. Check your answers with a partner.

1. _____   **2.** _____

3. _____   **4.** _____

5. _____   **6.** _____

7. _____   **8.** _____

EXERCISE 7: Discuss Your Expectations 2

A. Listen again to Conversation 2 and answer the questions with a partner.

1. What did the man, Harry, learn about Angela?

2. What did Angela learn about Harry?

3. Do you think Harry is older or about the same age as Angela? Why do you think so?

4. Do you believe his story about his computer? Why or why not?

5. Will there be some trouble? What do you think will happen?

B. Rewrite the second half of the conversation so that Angela avoids possible trouble. Use your own paper.

Harry: <u>Maybe you can help me. What's your name?</u> _____

Angela: _____

STEP 3: Speaking

EXERCISE 8: Define Types of Comments

A. Create definitions with your class of "appropriate comments" and "inappropriate comments." Write the definitions in the blanks.

Appropriate Comments: _____

_____

Inappropriate Comments: _____

_____

B. List situations or people with whom we . . .

1. . . . must be appropriate: _____

_____

2. . . . can be inappropriate: _____

_____

EXERCISE 9: Identify Appropriateness

Write "app" for "appropriate" or "inapp" for "inappropriate" in front of the comments. (Hint: Four of them are "inappropriate.")

_____ **1.** "No, I don't need any help, but thanks anyway."

_____ **2.** "Hi! What's your name? You are very nice-looking. Where do you live?"

_____ **3.** "I know you already have a boyfriend, but how about going on a date with me?"

_____ **4.** "You were a big help. Thanks a lot."

_____ **5.** "Thanks for the gift of the new shirt, but I already have a shirt in the same color."

_____ **6.** "Your shoes are completely weird!"

_____ **7.** "Your shoes are very interesting!"

EXERCISE 10: Analyze the Conversations

Answer these questions about Conversations 1 and 2 with a small group.

Conversation 1: A Study Plan

1. What part of Pam and Mike's conversation was appropriate?

2. What part of their conversation was inappropriate?

3. What could Pam do to change the situation?

Conversation 2: A Problem with a Computer

1. What could Harry do to change the situation on the bus?

2. How could Angela react in a different way to Harry on the bus?

Online Study Center   **Improve Your Grade**

STEP 4: Stepping It Up

EXERCISE 11: Create Expectations from Pictures

With a partner, discuss these questions for each picture in Exercise 12.

1. Where are the people in the picture?

2. What is the relationship of the people in the picture?

3. What do you think the people are talking about?

4. Are they saying something appropriate or inappropriate?

EXERCISE 12: **Identify Conversations**

Listen to the recording and match each picture with a conversation.

   1. Picture 1 is Conversation _____ .

   2. Picture 2 is Conversation _____ .

   3. Picture 3 is Conversation _____ .

   4. Picture 4 is Conversation _____ .

   5. Picture 5 is Conversation _____ .

EXERCISE 13: **Explain the Appropriateness**

Listen again to the recording for Exercise 12. With a small group, decide if the conversations are appropriate or inappropriate and explain why. Share your answers with the class.

Circle One   **Why?**

Conversation 1: Appropriate or Inappropriate   _____

Conversation 2: Appropriate or Inappropriate   _____

Conversation 3: Appropriate or Inappropriate   _____

Conversation 4: Appropriate or Inappropriate   _____

Conversation 5: Appropriate or Inappropriate   _____

EXERCISE 14: Prepare the Project

Form a small "observation" group. Your goal is to observe and listen as an anthropologist (a scientist who studies social behavior). You will observe small-group interaction in a public place. Go to the student center on your campus, a shopping mall, or a community center. Decide where and when you will go together to do your observation. The observation is described in detail in Chapter 3 and at the end of this unit.

My group members are: _____

We will go to: _____

Day: _____

Time: _____

EXERCISE 15: Evaluate Your Learning

A. Mark each item about your learning. Check (✓) True if you improved or False if you did not.

True   False

☐   ☐   **1.** I focused my listening on specific information.

☐   ☐   **2.** I created expectations for listening.

☐   ☐   **3.** I understood the details in casual conversation.

☐   ☐   **4.** I identified appropriate and inappropriate comments and situations.

B. Write about how you can identify a troubling conversation and how you can respond to one.

_____

_____

_____

_____

_____

Online Study Center   **ACE the Test!**

LET'S SAY THE RIGHT THING

Listening Focus: Problem Solving

Ask Yourself
Is it easy to ask for things that you need in English?

STEP 1: Pre-Listening

K
N
O
W
L
E
D
G
E

EXERCISE 1: Discuss Warm-Up Questions

Discuss with a small group. Write some of your answers on a separate piece of paper and share them with your class.

1. What is a compliment?
2. Do you often give compliments to other people?
3. Choose a person in your group and give that person a compliment.
4. What compliment(s) do you like to get from other people?
5. In other countries, what kinds of compliments do people give?
6. Tell about a compliment that someone gave you recently.

Online Study Center   **Prepare for Class**

EXERCISE 2: Preview Vocabulary

Match the expressions to their meanings.

_____ **1.** You hit the nail on the head.	**a.** What is happening?
_____ **2.** a bit	**b.** skin returns to normal
_____ **3.** What's up?	**c.** yearly celebration; a special event
_____ **4.** borrow	**d.** I'm curious.
_____ **5.** skin clears up	**e.** difficult
_____ **6.** I was wondering.	**f.** use and then return
_____ **7.** tough	**g.** I agree completely.
_____ **8.** anniversary	**h.** a little

 Guess the Idiom

If we "butter up" mom, she'll take us to the movies.

    a. If we interrupt mom, she'll take us to the movies.
    b. If we get mom dirty and greasy, she'll take us to the movies.
    c. If we give mom praise or a gift, she'll take us to the movies.

EXERCISE 3: Practice the Expressions

Fill in the blanks with the expressions from Exercise 2.

1. If you say "_____," it means that you agree with someone's comment or opinion.

2. If you _____ a car, you use it and then return it to its owner.

3. If you meet a friend, you might say, "_____?"

4. If you say, "I am _____ tired," you mean that you have only a little energy.

5. If you are celebrating your first _____, you have been married for 1 year.

6. If you hear, "The science class is _____," it means the class is hard or difficult.

7. If you say, "_____," then you want to ask someone a question.

8. If your _____, then your skin returns to normal.

STEP 2: Listening

C O M P R E H E N S I O N

LISTENING STRATEGY

Confirm an Expectation

Confirming an expectation helps you enter a conversation. You will need to take some time to listen to the conversation. After a few comments, be ready to say something. Follow these steps:

1. Think about what you will hear; in other words, create an expectation.
    a. Who is talking?
    b. What are they talking about?
    c. What do you know about the topic?
2. Think about how you can respond.
    a. If your expectation is *correct*, and you know what they are talking about, add your agreement and a statement.
    b. If your expectation is incorrect, ask a question to get more information.

EXERCISE 4: Create and Confirm Expectations

For each situation, read and discuss possible answers to the Pre-Listening Questions with a small group. Then listen to the recording of the Conversations and discuss your answers to the Post-Listening Questions.

SITUATION 1: Tracey is calling Devin. She met him in a computer science class. It seems that Devin knows a lot about computers. Tracey would like some help with the homework assignments for the class.

Pre-Listening

1. What question will Tracey ask first to start the conversation?
2. How will Tracey introduce herself to Devin?
3. How will she try to convince Devin to help her?

Post-Listening

4. Did you hit the nail on the head? In other words, is it what your group expected? Yes or no?
5. Do you think Tracy's comments were appropriate or inappropriate?
6. What would you say to convince Devin?

SITUATION 2: Marilyn's sister, Evelyn, just had a baby. Evelyn sent Marilyn a picture of her baby by e-mail. Marilyn got the picture but was surprised. Her new nephew is not very cute. Marilyn decides to call her sister.

Pre-Listening

1. How will Marilyn start the conversation?
2. What will Marilyn say about the picture of Evelyn's new baby?
3. Will Marilyn's comment be appropriate or inappropriate?

Post-Listening

4. Is it what your group expected? Yes or no?
5. Do you think Marilyn's comment was appropriate or inappropriate?
6. What are other things you could say about the baby?

SITUATION 3: Darryl wants to borrow Jim's car because he wants to take his girlfriend, Jenny, on a date Friday. He can't borrow his parents' car because they are using it. Darryl calls Jim to ask about his car. He tries hard to butter him up.

Pre-Listening

1. How will Darryl start the conversation?

2. What topic will Darryl talk about before he asks Jim about his car?

3. How will Jim react when Darryl suggests a plan to go out together?

Post-Listening

Now, listen to the telephone conversation between Darryl and Jim.

4. Is it what your group expected? Yes or no?

5. Do you think Darryl's way of asking was appropriate or inappropriate?

6. What would you say to convince Jim?

EXERCISE 5: Listen for Convincing Phrases

Listen again to the recording for Exercise 4 and answer these questions with your group.

1. What did Tracey say to convince Devin?

   _____

2. What did Marilyn say to her sister that was inappropriate?

   _____

3. What did Darryl say to try to convince Jim? Did it work? Why or why not?

   _____

STEP 3: Speaking

SPEAKING STRATEGY

Persuade Others

In Chapter 1, you practiced adding agreement to help another person feel comfortable. Complimenting is another way. Giving compliments can also help you persuade (or convince) someone to help you.

Here are some steps for persuading another person to help you:

1. Find a topic to agree about so that you both feel comfortable.
2. Give the person a compliment to show your appreciation.
3. Explain the kind of help that you need.
4. Ask for help.

EXERCISE 6: Persuade Others

With a partner, use expressions from the chart and fill in the missing lines in the monologues below.

Compliment	Need	Request
You are really . . .	I really need to . . .	Can you help me?
You are so good with (a noun) . . . You are good at (verb +ing) . . .	I could really use your help with . . .	Could you help me?
		Could you give me some suggestions?
I heard that you know all about . . .	You really know . . .	Do you have a few minutes to help me?
They say that you are good at . . .	I need to do . . .	Could you take some time to help me?

SITUATION 1: Tony wants to move the furniture in his dorm room. He says to his friend, Joe:

Compliment:	Joe, you're really strong.
Need:	I need some help moving a big desk.
Request:	_____

SITUATION 2: Joan bought her first computer and connected it to the Internet. She says to her classmate, Tina:

Compliment:	Tina, _____.
Need:	I need to e-mail my brother.
Request:	Do you have a few minutes to help me?

SITUATION 3: Ben doesn't know how to change the oil in his car. He says to his neighbor, Ken:

Compliment:	Ken, I heard you know all about cars.
Need:	_____
Request:	Could you take some time to show me how to do it?

SITUATION 4:

Compliment:	Gina, you are so good at shopping.
Need:	I need to buy a gift for my mother's birthday.
Request:	_____

SITUATION 5:

Compliment:	_____
Need:	I need to borrow a couple of bucks until Friday.
Request:	Could you help me with a loan?

SITUATION 6:

Compliment:	Lynn, I heard you're good at math.
Need:	_____
Request:	Do you have a few minutes to help me with this homework problem?

SITUATION 7:

Compliment:	Wow! You have a really cool car, Tom.
Need:	_____
Request:	_____

SITUATION 8:

Compliment:	_____
Need:	_____
Request:	Could you help me buy a new computer?

EXERCISE 7: **Persuade Others in Monologues**

A. In small groups, spread out the cut-up pieces of the persuasion monologues from Appendix 1 (page 153).

B. Work together and divide the pieces into three groups, with all Compliments together, all Needs together, and all Requests together.

C. Match each Compliment with a Need and a Request to create monologues.

D. When you are finished, double check your matches by reading the monologues aloud to each other.

Part 1	Part 2	Part 3
Compliment	Need	Request

EXERCISE 8: **Get Classmates' Information**

Ask the questions in the chart of three classmates. Fill in their responses. (You will use this information in Exercise 9.)

Student Name:			
1. What is your favorite subject in school?			
2. What do you like to do in your free time?			
3. Where do you shop for clothes?			

Online Study Center   **Improve Your Grade**

STEP 4: **Stepping It Up**

EXERCISE 9: **Put Together the Persuasions**

For Parts A through D, use the information from Exercise 8. Do not show your answers until Part D.

Example:

Part A: Melissa, you're so good at chemistry.

Part B: I need some help with my chemistry report.

Part C: Do you have some time to help me?

PART A: COMPLIMENTING OTHERS

Write a compliment for each person that you talked with.

Student Name	Compliment

PART B: STATING A NEED

Look at the compliment you wrote for each person. Imagine something that you need from each one. Write your need.

Student Name	Something I Need from Them

PART C: REQUESTING HELP

Look at the compliment and the need that you wrote for each person. Write your request for each one.

Student Name	My Request from Them for Help

PART D: GOING FOR HELP

Go to these students and tell them your compliment, your need, and your request. They should answer you appropriately.

Student Name	Their Response to Me

EXERCISE 10: Listen to a TV Comedy

A. Watch and listen to a TV comedy show.

B. At each commercial break, do the following. (Hint: Do not wait until the end of the show.):

    1. In the chart, write what is happening in the story. (Copy the chart on a separate piece of paper if you need more space.)

    2. Write what you think will happen *next* (as your prediction).

C. Listen to confirm your expectation. Write whether you were correct.

NAME OF THE TV SHOW: _____

What is happening?	What will happen next?	Were you correct? (Yes or No)
Commercial Break		
Commercial Break		

D. Describe the show you watched and share your notes in a small group.

EXERCISE 11: Prepare the Project

A. Watch as people greet each other and talk in a public place. Answer these questions as you observe. One or two students from your group should take notes while the others observe, and then change jobs. (Copy the chart on a separate piece of paper if you need more space.)

Show your instructor your notes when you are finished. At the end of this unit, there are more guidelines for this project.

OBSERVATION CHART: SOCIAL BEHAVIOR

Place: _____   Time: _____   Date: _____

	Observation 1	Observation 2
1. How many people are in the group?		
2. How do they greet each other?		
3. Do they touch? How about hug, shake hands, or kiss?		
4. How often do they ask questions of each other? (Count how many questions they ask.)		
5. Do they nod or smile while talking?		
6. How close are they to each other? Are they side by side, across from each other, in a circle, or in a line?		
7. Are they standing up or sitting down while they talk?		
8. How long do they talk?		
9. About what age are they? What age group are they, for example, children, teens, young adults, middle-aged adults, senior citizens?		
10. Do you think these people are family, friends, strangers, or a mixture?		

B. Think about a country that you are familiar with.

11. What would be different from what you observed?

12. What would be the same as what you observed?

EVALUATION

EXERCISE 12: Evaluate Your Learning

A. Mark all the boxes that apply to your learning.

- ☐ I learned to confirm my expectations.
- ☐ I learned how to compliment someone.
- ☐ I learned how to tell someone what I need.
- ☐ I learned how to request help of someone so that I get it.

B. Think about what was the most enjoyable part of this chapter for you. Write at least three sentences.

_____

_____

_____

_____

_____

_____

Online Study Center **ACE the Test!**

Online Teaching Center **Unit Assessment**

Instructors: Print out the unit assessment. Play the appropriate assessment recording for the class.

PROJECT
Cultural Anthropology

S Y N T H E S I S

Goal

You will focus your listening on specific information and learn how everyday people ask questions of strangers and keep a conversation going.

Description

You will observe and listen as an anthropologist (a scientist who studies social behavior). Take notes on your observations. At the end, you will discuss your results with your class. An Assessment Chart is at the end of this project.

Preparation 1: Organize Your Group

See Chapter 2, Exercise 14.

Preparation 2: Observe and Take Notes

See Chapter 3, Exercise 11.

Presentation and Discussion

After all the groups have completed their observations, discuss them as a class. Make as many generalizations (statements about what most groups observed) as possible.

   Make a chart in your classroom that is similar to the sample below. Write down the generalizations and fill in which groups observed each one.

   In U.S. culture, how do people generally act as friends in public places? And how do people generally act with strangers?

GENERALIZATIONS CHART

Friends	Strangers	Group making the observation
Wave and say "Hi"	Look at each other but don't talk	
Stop and talk	Do not touch each other	

Feedback

As a whole class, discuss the following questions.

1. Did you participate in the research, the note-taking (while observing), the presenting, and the discussion? What did you like doing the best?

2. Did you find any surprising results from your observations? If so, what were they?

Assessment Chart

Your instructor will use the following rubric to assess your work throughout the project.

Group Members:					
Criteria	**0** **None of the Time**	**2** **Some of the Time**	**3** **Most of the Time**	**4** **All of the Time**	**Comments**
1. Observation and Notes Did each student participate in the observation of at least two social interactions?					
2. Generalization Did these students interact and discuss their observations with the class?					
3. Feedback Did each student add something to the discussion?					
4. Respect Did these students encourage and support each other?					
Total Points:					

BUYING A COMPUTER

Content Area:
Computer Science

Skills You Will Learn

In this unit, you will:

Identify computer vocabulary.

Recognize main ideas.

Listen for definitions in context.

Understand comparison definitions.

Talk about using a computer.

Distinguish Yes/No and WH question types.

Use expressions to ask for information.

Listen to details and double check information.

Use natural intonation for questions.

Discuss with others possible solutions to a problem.

Online Study Center

http://college.hmco.com/pic/teskeone1e

WHAT IS A PERSONAL COMPUTER?

Listening Focus: Mini-Lecture

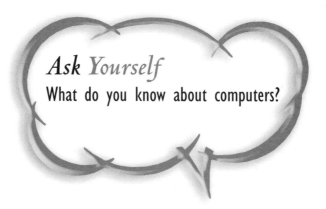

Ask Yourself
What do you know about computers?

STEP 1: Pre-Listening

K
N
O
W
L
E
D
G
E

EXERCISE 1: Discuss Warm-Up Questions

Discuss with a small group. Write some of your answers and share them with your class.

1. Do you like computers? Why or why not?
2. How do you use computers now?
3. What would you like to learn about computers? Why?
4. What do you think future computers will do that is different from today?
5. If you could buy a new computer today, what kind would you buy?
6. Do you ever read computer magazines? If so, what kind of information do you like to read about?

Online Study Center   **Prepare for Class**

EXERCISE 2: Preview Vocabulary 1

Label the computer below with these expressions: *tower, keyboard, monitor, mouse, 3.5-inch floppy disk drive,* and *CD-Rom drive.*

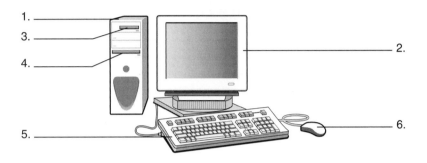

EXERCISE 3: Preview Vocabulary 2

Fill in the blanks with the appropriate words.

gamer	affordable	virus	download
moderate	performance	mid-range	
tech support	multimedia	document	

1. Ying-Li will _____ (v.) a lot of music for the Internet. Her newest **download** (n.) of classical music was some of the best.

2. My new car **performs** (v.) like an old truck. I will work on it to improve its _____ (n.).

3. Tom is crazy about playing advanced **games** (n.) on his computer. He is called a _____ (n.).

4. Jane **moderates** (v.) her game purchases. She buys games only at _____ (adj.) prices.

5. Antonio likes to play **multimedia** (adj.) programs on his computer. He then creates _____ (n.) for his website with digital music, photos, and video.

6. Antonio also **technologically** (adv.) **supports** (v.) other people on the Internet. His _____ _____ (compound n.) is very cheap to purchase.

7. Rosa cannot **afford** (v.) expensive computer games, so she finds _____ (adj.) games at discount stores.

8. Computer **viruses** (n.) can hurt any PC, so _____ (adj.) protection is important for every computer.

9. Mr. Chen **documents** (v.) his budget on the computer. Then he can easily check any _____ (n.) that he has made.

10. Mr. Chen did not need an expensive PC, so he bought one in the **middle** (adj.) **range** (n.) of the choices that were available. His _____ (adj.) computer works very well for him.

STEP 2: Listening

COMPREHENSION

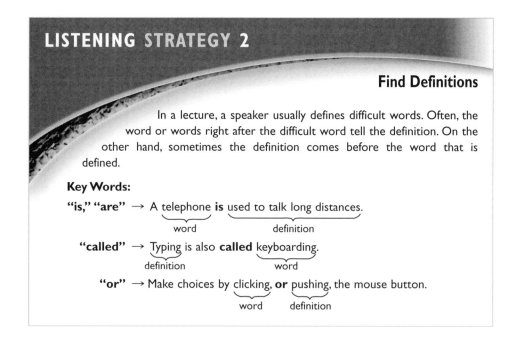

LISTENING STRATEGY 1

Listen for the Main Idea

"Main" means the same as "most important." Conversations do not always have "main ideas." In a conversation, people may talk about many ideas.

However, lectures usually have a main idea. If you can find the main idea, it will be easier to understand the lecture. How will you recognize the main idea?

In an organized lecture, the instructor usually begins by saying the main idea. In other words, she "introduces" the topic. Then she tells you the details about the main idea. This is the "body" of the lecture. At the end, she usually repeats the main idea in a "conclusion." Lectures have these parts:

Introduction → tells the main idea

Body → explains the details about the main idea

Conclusion → repeats the main idea

EXERCISE 4: Recognize Main Ideas

 Listen to "Mini-Lecture 1: Introduction to Computers." Choose the main idea of the *whole* mini-lecture.

A. Software tells the computer what to do.

B. Hardware and software are important parts of every computer.

C. Hardware is any part of the computer that we can touch.

LISTENING STRATEGY 2

Find Definitions

In a lecture, a speaker usually defines difficult words. Often, the word or words right after the difficult word tell the definition. On the other hand, sometimes the definition comes before the word that is defined.

Key Words:

"is," "are" → A telephone **is** used to talk long distances.
                  word   definition

"called" → Typing is also **called** keyboarding.
              definition   word

"or" → Make choices by clicking, **or** pushing, the mouse button.
                       word   definition

EXERCISE 5: Listen for Definitions

Listen again to Mini-Lecture 1. Fill in the words that match the definitions.

1. The parts of the computer you can touch are called _____.

2. Something that lets you see information is called the _____.

3. Something that lets you move around "inside" the computer is called the _____.

4. Something that contains the "brain" of the computer is called the _____.

5. Something that tells the computer what to do is called _____.

EXERCISE 6: Make Your Own Definitions

Write two sentences on any topic. In each, use a key word from Listening Strategy 2. Share with a partner.

1. _____

2. _____

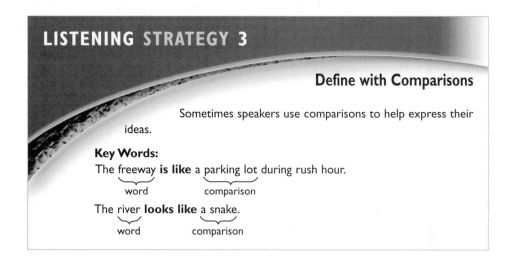

LISTENING STRATEGY 3

Define with Comparisons

Sometimes speakers use comparisons to help express their ideas.

Key Words:

The freeway **is like** a parking lot during rush hour.
        word   comparison

The river **looks like** a snake.
       word   comparison

Example 1:

COMPUTER PROCESSOR: A computer processor is like a human's brain.

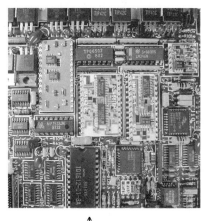

=

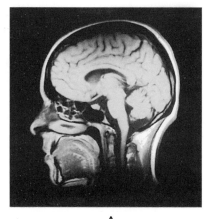

a computer processor   a human's brain

Example 2:

COMPUTER MOUSE: A computer mouse looks like a mouse with a long tail.

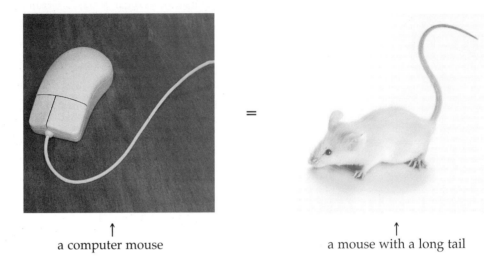

↑   ↑
a computer mouse   a mouse with a long tail

EXERCISE 7: Match the Comparisons

 Listen to the recording. Write the definition letter that matches each computer part.

Definition Letter	Computer Part
_____	**1.** software
_____	**2.** different types of drives
_____	**3.** monitor
_____	**4.** keyboard
_____	**5.** tower

EXERCISE 8: Make Comparison Definitions

Make two comparison definitions with key words from Listening Strategy 3. Share with a partner.

1. _____

2. _____

EXERCISE 9: Recognize Main Ideas

 Listen to "Mini-Lecture 2: Buying a Personal Computer." Write the main idea. (Hint: The speaker explains it in the introduction and conclusion.)

You should _____

EXERCISE 10: Un**l**derstand Details

Listen again to Mini-Lecture 2. Match the parts of the sentences.

_____ **1.** "Surfing the Net" means . . .

_____ **2.** PC means . . .

_____ **3.** Word-processing is also called . . .

_____ **4.** The most expensive computers are used for . . .

_____ **5.** Basic computers are used for . . .

a. . . . personal computer.

b. . . . Internet, e-mail, and word-processing.

c. . . . searching for information on the Internet.

d. . . . keyboarding.

e. . . . digital video.

EXERCISE 11: Listen for Details

Listen again to Mini-Lecture 2. Write the uses for different types of computers. Copy the chart on a separate piece of paper if you need more space.

Types of Computers	Uses
Basic PCs	
Mid-range PCs	
Expensive PCs	

EXERCISE 12: Make Comparisons

Listen again to the recording for Mini-Lecture 2 and complete the mini-lecture comparisons on the left. Use your own ideas to create different comparisons on the right.

	Mini-Lecture Comparison	My Comparison
1. Buying a computer without doing research first . . .		
2. Cheap and affordable PCs . . . are like farm trucks.		
3. A mid-range PC . . .		
4. The most expensive computers . . .		

A P P L I C A T I O N

STEP 3: Speaking

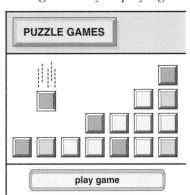

EXERCISE 13: Talk about Using a Computer

Use ideas from both mini-lectures. Create short conversations about each picture. The first line of each conversation is here for you. Share your conversations when you are finished.

Example:

Yuki:	What are you doing?
Johan:	I am making a digital video to send to Kim.
Yuki:	What is the video about?
Johan:	Kim and I went on vacation in Canada. I have some great digital photos that I am putting together with music.

1. Who are you e-mailing?

2. What game are you playing?

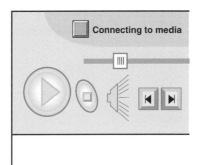

3. What are you listening to?

4. What are you searching for on the Internet?

5. What are you downloading?

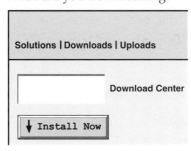

6. Are you finished typing your homework?

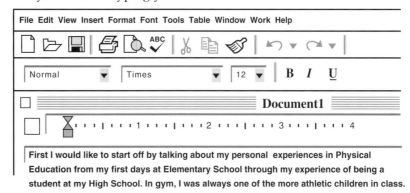

EXERCISE 14: Show Your Knowledge

A. Make small groups. Each group uses one complete set of the cut-up computer-vocabulary game pieces from Appendix 2 (page 157). Turn the pieces face-down on a desk and divide them among the group members.

B. Take turns drawing pictures of the vocabulary. Other members guess what the student artist is drawing. The artist cannot talk, signal, or act.

C. When you are finished, share your pictures with your classmates.

 ## EXERCISE 15: Practice Speaking for TOEFL® Success

Give and support your opinion about how we can use a computer or the Internet. You have 1 minute. Talk about only one or two main ideas. Here are some questions to guide you:

- How do you feel about computers? Why?
- How do you use a computer?
- What is interesting about computers or the Internet?

Online Study Center   **Improve Your Grade**

STEP 4: Stepping It Up

A N A L Y S I S

EXERCISE 16: Understand through Comparisons

A. Look at advertisements for computers in newspapers, magazines catalogues, and online.

B. As a class, define these two words:

Inexpensive PCs cost _____.

Expensive PCs cost _____.

C. Compare inexpensive PCs to expensive PCs. Use information from the mini-lectures, your personal knowledge, and computer advertisements to complete the chart.

Inexpensive computers . . .	Expensive computers . . .
1.	1.
2.	2.
3.	3.
4.	4.
5.	5.
6.	6.
7.	7.

E V A L U A T I O N

EXERCISE 17: Evaluate Your Learning

Check all of the items that you have learned how to do in this chapter.

☐ Recognize main ideas

☐ Define computer vocabulary

☐ Listen for definitions in context

☐ Understand comparison definitions

Online Study Center   **ACE the Test!**

SHOPPING FOR A COMPUTER

Listening Focus: Conversation

Ask Yourself
What are some reasons to buy a computer?

STEP 1: Pre-Listening

KNOWLEDGE

EXERCISE 1: Discuss Warm-Up Questions

Discuss with a small group. Write some of your answers and share them with your class.

1. Do you own your own computer?

2. Have you ever shopped for computers? How much do they cost?

3. Do you think it is a good idea to have your own computer, or is it better to use the computers on campus or in the neighborhood library?

4. Tell about a bad experience that you had with a computer recently.

5. Are you interested in taking computer science courses in the future?

Online Study Center   **Prepare for Class**

EXERCISE 2: Preview Vocabulary

Match the expressions to their meanings.

_____	**1.** tight budget	**a.** written agreement to fix something
_____	**2.** mid-price	**b.** the part where the sound comes out
_____	**3.** range	**c.** not much money to spend
_____	**4.** standard feature	**d.** medium price
_____	**5.** warranty	**e.** something included with the product
_____	**6.** afford	**f.** the place you pay for items in a store
_____	**7.** register	**g.** a variety of things, such as prices
_____	**8.** speakers	**h.** have enough money for something

Guess the Idiom

This computer costs "an arm and a leg."

    a. This computer costs the same as if I sell my arm and leg.

    b. This computer costs the same as a visit to the doctor.

    c. This computer costs a large amount of money.

EXERCISE 3: Preview Project Vocabulary

Choose True or False for each definition. Use a dictionary to check your answers if you are not sure.

True   False   **1. Brainstorm** means to say or write many ideas as quickly as possible.

True   False   **2.** A **deadline** is the date when you must finish something.

True   False   **3. Responsibilities** are things that are not necessary to do.

True   False   **4. Prepare** means to not get ready.

True   False   **5. Tasks** are jobs, or actions, to do.

EXERCISE 4: Get People's Responses

Answer Questions 1, 2, and 3 in the chart and ask three other people. Check (✓) everyone's answers and the most common ones.

		Me				Most Common Answers
		Names				
1.	How well do you use the computer?					
	I'm a beginner.					
	I'm about average.					
	I'm pretty good.					
2.	How much money could you spend on a computer?					
	I'm on a tight budget.					
	I'm looking for something in the mid-price range.					
	It's okay if it costs an arm and a leg.					
3.	How do you (or would you) use your computer? (Rank your choices as 1st, 2nd, 3rd, etc.)					
	Surfing the Internet					
	Making digital video movies					
	Playing computer games					
	Listening to music					
	Sending e-mail					
	Doing homework assignments					
	Other: _____					

STEP 2: Listening

C
O
M
P
R
E
H
E
N
S
I
O
N

LISTENING STRATEGY

Ask for Information

Yes/No questions begin with a verb. They ask for only a "yes" or "no" answer.

Can this computer come with software for editing movies?

Are there any other computers for the same price?

WH questions begin with question words that ask for specific information. Question words include *What, When, Where, Why,* and *How*.

Why do you want a new computer?

How many features does this computer have?

EXERCISE 5: Identify Question Types

Write "WH" for WH Questions and "Y/N" for Yes/No questions.

__WH__ **1.** What do you do with your computer?

_____ **2.** Do you want a CD drive?

_____ **3.** Where can I buy an inexpensive one?

_____ **4.** Sir, can you help me?

_____ **5.** When does this store close?

_____ **6.** How much is this computer?

_____ **7.** Does your store have any less-expensive computers?

_____ **8.** Is there a warranty with the purchase price?

_____ **9.** Why is this computer so much more expensive?

_____ **10.** Who repairs computers in your store?

EXERCISE 6: Listen for Questions 1

A. Listen to "Conversation 1: How Can I Help You?" Write all the questions that you hear.

B. Identify Y/N and WH question types.

C. Identify the speakers as "S" for Salesman or "C" for customer.

Questions		Y/N or WH	Speakers
1. _____ ?		_____	_____
2. _____ ?		_____	_____
3. _____ ?		_____	_____
4. _____ ?		_____	_____
5. _____ ?		_____	_____

EXERCISE 7: Listen for Comprehension

 A. Listen again to Conversation 1. Answer the questions. Check your answers with a partner.

   1. What did the salesman ask the customer first?

   2. Why do you think the salesman says that the customer came to the right place?

   3. What does she do on her old computer?

   4. What additional feature does she want on a new computer? Is that a standard feature?

B. Create expectations for the next conversation. Write three WH questions and two Y/N questions that the salesman and customer could ask.

   5. _____

   6. _____

   7. _____

   8. _____

   9. _____

LISTENING STRATEGY

Double Check the Details

Sometimes we need to make sure that we understand every detail. But we don't want to ask someone to repeat everything that was just said. So, we ask for only the part that we didn't understand. In order to double check the details:

1. Paraphrase the information that you understood.

2. Ask only about the piece of information that you didn't understand.

Useful Expressions:

I understood [. . .], but what did you mean by [. . .]?

When you said [. . .], did you mean [. . .]?

Let me see if I have this right. So far, you said that [. . .].

What was the last thing that you said?

I got most of that, but I didn't understand [. . .].

A P P L I C A T I O N

EXERCISE 8: Listen for Questions 2

A. Listen to "Conversation 2: Is There Anything Else?" Write all the questions that you hear.

B. Identify Y/N and WH question types.

C. Identify the speakers as "S" for Salesman and "C" for customer.

Questions	Y/N or WH	Speakers
1. _____?	_____	_____
2. _____?	_____	_____
3. _____?	_____	_____
4. _____?	_____	_____
5. _____?	_____	_____
6. _____?	_____	_____
7. _____?	_____	_____
8. _____?	_____	_____

EXERCISE 9: Listen for Double Checking

 Listen again to the recording for Conversation 2. Answer these questions. (Hint: See Listening Strategy 2 to review useful expressions.)

1. At the beginning of the conversation, what did the salesman say to double check on what the customer wants?
2. What did the customer say to double check her understanding about the warranty?
3. What did the customer say to double check her understanding about tech support?

STEP 3: Speaking

EXERCISE 10: Organize a Conversation

With a partner, choose lines from the columns to create a conversation between a salesman and a customer at a computer store. Use your imagination and add more lines.

Salesman	Customer
Is there anything else?	Can you help me find ...?
Sure. About how much money do you want to spend?	Does this come with ...?
Let me see if I have this right. You said that ...	I got most of that, but I didn't understand....
Is there a particular kind of computer that you like?	I'm on a tight budget.
	What was the last thing that you said?
Okay, great. Well, let's look at....	Oh, I don't care if it costs an arm and a leg. I just want....
What else will you use it for?	I really like....
Sure, all of our computers come with....	When you said ..., did you mean ...?
	What time do you close?

Online Study Center   **Improve Your Grade**

STEP 4: Stepping It Up

SYNTHESIS

EXERCISE 11: Talk about Shopping

A. Find pictures of hardware and/or software that you would like to buy. Draw or paste pictures of two items here. Create a conversation in which you are buying and selling your items. Ask specific questions and use computer vocabulary.

Picture of Item 1:	Picture of Item 2:

Salesman: Hi. _____

Customer: Yes, I _____

Salesman: _____

Customer: _____

Salesman: _____

Customer: _____

Salesman: _____

B. Optional: Go to a real store and discuss computers. It is not necessary to buy anything. You can tell the salesperson, "I am just looking."

EXERCISE 12: Prepare the Project

Listen to the recording. Use expressions from Chapter 5, Exercise 3 to fill in the information about the project. In Chapter 6, Exercise 10, you will do the project. At the end of this unit, there are more guidelines for the project.

1. What are the things that your group will need to do?

Make a list of _____

2. Who will do each part? What part will you do?

Decide each group member's _____

3. Where will you find the supplies?

_____ ideas for places to find the supplies and materials that you need.

4. When do you need to have the items ready?

Make a _____ for finishing each step.

5. When will you practice?

_____ and practice individually and as a group.

E
V
A
L
U
A
T
I
O
N

EXERCISE 13: **Evaluate Your Learning**

A. In this chapter, write two things that you learned about listening and speaking.

   1. I learned how to understand _____ .

   2. I learned how to talk (or ask) about _____ .

B. Think about what was the most enjoyable part of this chapter for you. Write at least three sentences.

_____

_____

_____

_____

_____

 *Online Study Center*   **ACE the Test!**

6

PROBLEMS BUYING A COMPUTER

Listening Focus: Problem Solving

Ask Yourself
What kind of problems have you had with a computer or other machine?

STEP 1: Pre-Listening

KNOWLEDGE

EXERCISE 1: Discuss Warm-Up Questions

Discuss with a small group. Write some of your answers and share them with your whole class.

1. What do you do *first* when you have a problem? Why?

2. When you have a problem, do you talk with another person? If so, whom?

3. Do you think you use good methods to solve your problems? Why or why not?

4. Tell a story about a problem you had that you solved successfully.

5. Tell about a problem you helped another person solve.

Prepare for Class

EXERCISE 2: Preview Vocabulary

Use your dictionary and write definitions for the words in **bold** print. Then close your dictionary and write an example sentence for each.

1. **Solution** means _____

   Example Sentence: _____

2. **Problem** means _____

   Example Sentence: _____

3. A computer **lab** is _____

   Example Sentence: _____

4. **Crowded** means _____

   Example Sentence: _____

5. **Accounting** means _____

   Example Sentence : _____

6. **Recommend** means _____

   Example Sentence: _____

7. **Worried** means _____

   Example Sentence: _____

8. **Prefer** means _____

   Example Sentence: _____

STEP 2: Listening

EXERCISE 3: Identify the Problem

 A. Before listening to "Problem Solving 1: Daniel's Problem," look at the photo on page 56. Answer these questions.

1. What does Daniel study?

2. What kind of problem could he have?

3. Does he own his own computer? How long has he owned it?

B. Listen to Problem Solving 1. Choose the sentence that best describes Daniel's situation.

4. Daniel wants to buy a new computer, but he does not have enough money.

5. Daniel is having trouble studying because the computer lab is noisy.

6. Daniel doesn't know what kind of computer to buy.

EXERCISE 4: Listen for Specific Information 1

 Listen again to Problem Solving 1. Answer the questions.

1. Who has the problem?

   _____ has the problem.

2. What subject is he studying in college?

   He is studying _____

3. Why does he have to wait to use computers at school?

   He waits for a computer at school because _____

4. When did he get his old computer?

   He got his computer in _____

5. Does he like his computer? Why or why not?

   _____

CULTURAL POINT

Find Solutions to Problems

In the United States, brainstorming is a very popular way to solve problems. Sometimes it is done independently, and sometimes it is done with the help of others.

The first step in solving a difficult situation is identifying the biggest part of the problem. The next step is brainstorming all of the possible solutions. In other words, talk about or write down every possibility—even if it seems strange. After brainstorming, try to choose the best solution for the situation. To solve a problem:

1. *Identify* the problem.
2. *Brainstorm* every possibility—even strange ones.
3. *Choose* the best solution.

Unfortunately, sometimes there isn't a perfect solution.

EXERCISE 5: Recognize and Solve Problems

In a small group, discuss these problem-solving steps about Daniel's situation. Give everyone in your group a chance to speak.

1. Identify Daniel's most important problem. _____
   _____

2. Brainstorm at least three possible solutions to his problem.
   a. _____
   b. _____
   c. _____

3. From your list, choose the best solution. Explain why your group thinks this is the best. _____
   _____

EXERCISE 6: Listen for Specific Information 2

 Listen to "Problem Solving 2: Daniel's Solution." Answer the questions.

1. Who does Daniel decide to talk to?
2. What are Daniel's professors telling him?
3. According to Daniel, what is the problem with his old computer?
4. How much would Daniel's new computer cost?
5. Who else will Daniel talk to?

STEP 3: Speaking

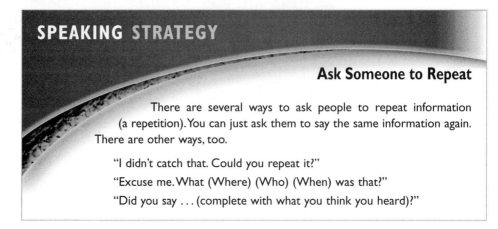

SPEAKING STRATEGY

Ask Someone to Repeat

There are several ways to ask people to repeat information (a repetition). You can just ask them to say the same information again. There are other ways, too.

"I didn't catch that. Could you repeat it?"

"Excuse me. What (Where) (Who) (When) was that?"

"Did you say . . . (complete with what you think you heard)?"

EXERCISE 7: Ask for a Repetition

Take turns asking for repetitions in the conversations below. Use the expressions in the Speaking Strategy.

Conversation 1

Person A:	My computer is too slow. I want to buy a new one.
Person B:	Excuse me. What _____
Person A:	I want to buy a new computer because my old one is slow.
Person B:	Oh. I bought a new computer last year. The monitor is really big.
Person A:	_____
Person B:	The monitor is 19 inches. That's really big.

Conversation 2

Person A:	I like sending e-mail to my friends.
Person B:	Did you say _____
Person A:	Yeah, to my friends. How about you?
Person B:	Sure, I send e-mail. I also enjoy surfing the Net.
Person A:	_____
Person B:	I like to surf the Net.

EXERCISE 8: Repeat with a Little Change

Create your own conversations by following this pattern:

1. Make a statement;

2. Ask for a repeat with a WH question **or** an expression from the Speaking Strategy; and

3. Repeat with a little change.

Example:

Person A:	*Make a statement* →	My favorite actor is Tom Cruise.
Person B:	*Ask to repeat* →	Excuse me. Who is your favorite actor?
Person A:	*Repeat with a little change* →	Tom Cruise is the best.

Conversation 1

Person A:	*Make a statement* →	My favorite magazine is _____.
Person B:	*Ask to repeat* →	Excuse me. What is your favorite magazine?
Person A:	*Repeat with a little change* →	_____.

Conversation 2

Person A:	*Make a statement* →	I really like _____.
Person B:	*Ask to repeat* →	I didn't catch that. _____ do you really like?
Person A:	*Repeat with a little change* →	_____.

Conversation 3

Person A:	*Make a statement* →	_____.
Person B:	*Ask to repeat* →	Did you say there's a 30-year warranty?
Person A:	*Repeat with a little change* →	_____.

Conversation 4

Person A:	*Make a statement* →	_____.
Person B:	*Ask to repeat* →	_____.
Person A:	*Repeat with a little change* →	_____.

Conversation 5

Person A:	*Make a statement* →	_____.
Person B:	*Ask to repeat* →	_____.
Person A:	*Repeat with a little change* →	_____.

☼ *Online Study Center*   **Improve Your Grade**

STEP 4: Stepping It Up

A N A L Y S I S

EXERCISE 9: Listen to a TV Comedy

Watch at least 30 minutes of a situation comedy show on TV in English. You may choose the same show that you saw in Chapter 3. Answer the questions in the chart.

NAME OF THE TV SHOW: _____

Questions	Answers
I. What is a problem that one of the characters has?	I.
2. Brainstorm ideas: How would you solve the problem? (Tell two different ways.)	2.
3. In the end, how did the character solve the problem?	3.
4. Is this solution really possible? Or is it only for TV? Why?	4.

EXERCISE 10: Prepare the Project

For the Unit Project, you will create a computer store. Form a group. Fill in the Action Plan below with names and deadlines. Use the receipts in Appendix 3 (page 159) and the Store Inventory form in Appendix 4 (page 161). When you do the "Preparation" step in the Action Plan, fill in a receipt for each item that you plan to sell. During your sale, you will give a receipt to every customer who buys something. At the end of your sale, you will fill in the Store Inventory form. At the end of this unit, there are more guidelines for the project.

ACTION PLAN

	What should you do?	Who is responsible for this?
Research	**1.** Find newspaper ads.	Person:
	2. Look on the Internet.	Person:
	3. Get a computer store catalogue.	Person:
	4. Collect more advertisements.	Person:
	Deadline for "Research":	
Preparation	**5.** Cut out photos from your research.	Person:　All team members
	6. Decide the cost of each item. On the receipts, fill in the prices of the items and attach them to the pictures so that your customers can see them when they go "shopping."	Person:　All team members
	7. Create a name for your store.	Person:　All team members
	Deadline for "Preparation":	
Practice	**8.** Put all of the photos and prices together on a table.	Person:
	9. Organize "your" computer store by grouping pictures together.	Person:
	10. Practice what you will say when you are the salesperson.	Person:　All team members
	11. Practice what you will say when you are the customer.	Person:　All team members
	Deadline for "Practice":	
Presentation	**12.** Sell your computers and computer parts to other students.	Person:　All team members
	13. Buy computers and computer parts from other students.	Person:　All team members
	Deadline for "Presentation":	

EXERCISE 11: Evaluate Your Learning

Mark each item about your learning as either True or False.

True   False 1. I can identify specific information, such as *who, what, when, where, why,* and *how.*

True   False 2. I can discuss possible solutions to a problem.

True   False 3. I can use several ways to ask someone to repeat something—not just say, "Please repeat that."

Online Study Center   **ACE the Test!**

Online Teaching Center   **Unit Assessment**

Instructors: Print out the unit assessment. Play the appropriate assessment recording for the class.

PROJECT

Make a Computer Store

S Y N T H E S I S

Goal

You will use computer vocabulary, ask for information, and double check information.

Description

You will create a computer store and take turns buying and selling computer items. You will use pictures of computers and computer parts that you find to make your store. Try to sell more equipment than the other groups. Try to use expressions from the whole unit.

Everyone in every group will be evaluated on the work that they do and how much English they use. An Assessment Chart is at the end of this project.

Preparation 1: Learn about Group Work

See Chapter 5, Exercise 14.

Preparation 2: Fill Out the Action Plan

See Chapter 6, Exercise 10.

Computer Store

Do your Action Plan. Make a computer store with the pictures that you find. Then your group will sell computers and computer parts to the other groups in your class. Try to sell more than the other groups.

Also, each group will have $5,000 US to purchase computers and computer parts from the other stores. You cannot buy anything from your own store. When you sell an item, fill in a receipt (from Appendix 3, page 159). Give half of it to your customer and keep the other half. When your sale is finished, fill in the Store Inventory form (from Appendix 4, page 161).

Feedback

How did your group do?
Did your group sell everything?
Did your group find a good deal?
What was helpful about this project?

Assessment Chart

Your instructor will use the following rubric to assess your work throughout the project.

Group Members:					
Criteria	**0** None of the Time	**2** Some of the Time	**3** Most of the Time	**4** All of the Time	**Comments**
1. Filled Out the Action Plan Did each group show the instructor a completed Action Plan?					
2. Group Work Did the students interact, discussing and asking questions?					
3. Language Did each student try to speak only English? Did they use expressions from the unit?					
4. Respect Did the students encourage and support each other?					
Total Points:					

BEING POPULAR

Content Area:
Psychology

Skills You Will Learn

In this unit, you will:

- Understand a comparison/contrast lecture.

- Take notes and fill in a T-Formation chart.

- Express opinions on a topic.

- Find out information online.

- Make suggestions in a conversation.

- Distinguish between agreeing and suggesting alternatives.

- Tell what you prefer to do.

- Listen for emotions in people's voices.

- Disagree without offending.

- Use idioms to express your feelings.

Online Study Center
http://college.hmco.com/pic/marcyone1e

OUR NEED TO BE POPULAR

Listening Focus: Mini-Lecture

Ask Yourself
What motivates you?
Why do you do what you do?

STEP I: Pre-Listening

KNOWLEDGE

EXERCISE I: Discuss Warm-Up Questions

Discuss with a small group. Write some of your group answers and share them with your class.

1. Is it easy to move away from home? What is easy about it? What is difficult about it?

2. Have you made friends from different cultures and different language backgrounds?

3. Do these "new" friends influence your behavior? How?

4. What do you think of Americans? Are they shy? Are they outgoing?

5. How about people in other countries? Are they shy or outgoing?

6. How do you prefer to be?

Online Study Center   **Prepare for Class**

EXERCISE 2: Preview Vocabulary

A. Fill in the verb forms of the nouns in the chart.

	Key Words		Meanings	
	Noun	**Verb**	**Noun**	**Verb**
1.	interaction	_____	response between two people	converse
2.	maturity	_____	growth and development	become more adult-like
3.	support	_____	help	help
4.	participation	_____	sharing in a group activity	join in and take part
5.	satisfaction	_____	comfortable feeling	meet a need or a desire

B. Fill in the sentences with expressions from the chart. Then write *noun* or *verb* for each expression.

verb **1.** Two people _____ when they talk and do things together.

_____ **2.** Children who play happily together have healthy _____.

_____ **3.** People show _____ if they are responsible and respond calmly to daily problems.

_____ **4.** Children usually _____ quickly if they lose their parents at a young age.

_____ **5.** John and his wife, Mimi, help each other and solve problems together. In other words, they give each other _____.

_____ **6.** In their marriage, John _____ Mimi, and Mimi _____ John.

_____ **7.** Language teachers want their students to _____ in every class.

_____ **8.** Daily _____ is usually part of the grade for a language class.

_____ **9.** At noon, I am hungry, so I _____ my need for food by eating something.

_____ **10.** If I must work through lunch, I do not have the _____ of eating a good meal.

STEP 2: Listening

COMPREHENSION

LISTENING STRATEGY

Take Notes in a T-Formation

Taking notes in a T-formation chart is helpful when you hear information that compares and contrasts information. A comparison shows similarity between two things. A contrast shows differences. Categories for the contrasting information can be listed on the left.

Categories	Topic I	Topic 2
_____		
_____		
_____		

EXERCISE 3: Do T-Formation Note-Taking

Copy the chart below on a separate piece of paper. Listen to the recording about two animals and take notes in your chart. Compare your notes with your classmates' notes.

Categories	Animal 1:_____	Animal 2:_____
Country		
Color		
Size		
Food		

EXERCISE 4: Find Definitions in a Mini-Lecture

Listen to "Mini-Lecture: Peer Relationships." Match the expressions in the mini-lecture to their meanings.

_____ 1. peers   **a.** unhappy

_____ 2. positive   **b.** teach, or train

___a___ 3. negative   **c.** happy

_____ 4. coach   **d.** able to make friends easily

_____ 5. sociable   **e.** people of the same age

EXERCISE 5: Take Notes in a T-Formation Chart

 Listen again to the Mini-Lecture. Fill in the missing information in the chart.

	Characteristics of	
Categories	**Popular People**	**Unpopular People**
Personality		shy and quiet
Friends		
Participation	join in many activities	
Talk		
Groups		good at working alone
Attitude		

STEP 3: Speaking

CULTURAL POINT

Soften Your Opinion

Americans do not hide their feelings very often. They tell their opinions. Everyone listens *even if* they do not like the opinion. Sometimes they worry that they might hurt someone's feelings. So, they "soften" their opinion by using phrases such as:

You may not agree with me, but I think *[that]*. . . .

I personally believe that. . . .

I think I have a little different view. I think *[that]*. . . .

You made a good point, but I personally feel that. . . .

I agree with what you said about. . . . *[followed by a gerund]*.

Example:

Sam:	You may not agree with me, but I think that we need to have more time to finish the project.
Sam's Boss:	You made a good point, but I personally feel that your team has enough time.
Becky:	I think I have a little different view. I think that Sam needs to participate more.
Lucy:	I agree with what Becky said about Sam participating. I also wish he could be more positive.
Sam:	I personally believe that I support the team a lot. However, you made a good point, and I will be more positive.
Sam's Boss:	*Great! This has been a good meeting.*

EXERCISE 6: Soften Your Opinion

Match these softening phrases with the rest of the sentences. A variety of matches are possible.

_____ **1.** I agree with what you said about . . .

_____ **2.** I personally believe that . . .

_____ **3.** You may not agree with me, but I think . . .

_____ **4.** In my opinion . . .

_____ **5.** You made a good point, but . . .

_____ **6.** I think I have a little different view.

a. people need to eat less fast food.

b. I think the tuition at this school is too cheap, especially for international students.

c. reading newspapers in English. It's hard.

d. I feel that the assignment is too easy.

e. we need fewer computer labs on campus.

f. that students should eat in the cafeteria every day.

EXERCISE 7: Express Opinions Softly

Complete the statements to express your opinion. Tell a partner your opinions softly.

In my opinion, *people are usually considerate.*

I personally feel *that people need to be more polite.*

_____ **1.** In my opinion . . . *people should not* _____

_____ **2.** I personally believe . . . *that the* _____ *government is* _____

_____ **3.** I personally think . . . *more* _____ *should* _____

_____ **4.** I personally feel . . . _____

_____ **5.** You may not agree with me, but _____

EXERCISE 8: Practice Speaking for TOEFL® Success

Give and support your opinion about spending money on friends. You have 1 minute. Talk about only one or two main ideas. Here are some questions to guide you:

Can you "buy" friends with money? Why or why not?

How much money is appropriate to spend on other people?

When is it appropriate to spend money on others?

EXERCISE 9: Exchange Opinions

Read the statements and discuss your opinions. Use the expressions from the Cultural Point.

Statement:	We should not look for our spouse among our peers.
Opinion 1:	I personally think that a husband or wife should be a peer.
Opinion 2:	You may not agree with me, but I think a husband should be older.

Statement:	Parents should choose the friends of their children.
Opinion 1:	I personally feel _____
Opinion 2:	I'm not sure. In my opinion, _____

Statement:	Shy people never succeed.
Opinion 1:	_____
Opinion 2:	_____

Statement:	Popular people have happier lives than people who are not so popular.
Opinion 1:	_____
Opinion 2:	_____

Statement:	Men mature more slowly than women.
Opinion 1:	_____
Opinion 2:	_____

Statement:	Sometimes anti-social people become popular.
Opinion 1:	_____
Opinion 2:	_____

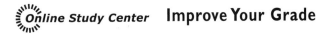 **Online Study Center**   **Improve Your Grade**

STEP 4: Stepping It Up

EXERCISE 10: Investigate Peer Relationships

Do research at the library or on the Internet about peer relationships. Share the results of your research with your class.

Research Questions:

1. What age group of people is discussed in the articles you found?
2. Can you find a sentence that defines "peer pressure"? Write it down.
3. What did you learn that is interesting?
4. Write one or two websites that look interesting for more information.

**E
V
A
L
U
A
T
I
O
N**

EXERCISE 11: Evaluate Your Learning

A. Mark these statements True or False about your learning.

True   False   **1.** I know how to take notes on a lecture that compares two things.

True   False   **2.** I know the ending of a noun is sometimes "-ion," e.g., interaction.

True   False   **3.** I understand how I can add my opinion to a conversation.

True   False   **4.** I learned something new about peer pressure.

B. Choose one of the items you marked "True." Write at least three sentences about what you learned.

_____

_____

_____

_____

 **Online Study Center   ACE the Test!**

LET'S PARTY!

Listening Focus:
Mini-Lecture

Ask Yourself
What do you like to do with your friends?

STEP 1: Pre-Listening

KNOWLEDGE

EXERCISE 1: Discuss Warm-Up Questions

Discuss your preferences about making suggestions with a partner.

1. Do you often make suggestions to do something with someone else?

2. When you want to make a suggestion to do something, how do you ask?

3. If that person does not want to do that, what do you say?

4. Do you usually do what *you* want to do?

5. Or do other people usually persuade you to do what *they* want to do?

6. Tell about a suggestion that you made recently.

Online Study Center   Prepare for Class

SPEAKING STRATEGY

Persuade Other People

Encouraging or pressuring someone to do what you want is called *persuasion*. To persuade another person, we make *suggestions*. Sometimes the other person may agree. Other times, that person may offer an alternative, or another idea.

Making Suggestions		Giving Alternatives	
Let's . . .	go to the library.	**I'd like to . . .**	go to Jan's party.
We could . . .	go to the movies.	**I'd rather . . .**	get something to eat.
Do you feel like . . .	hanging out at the mall?	**How about if we . . .**	go to the library?
Could we . . .	go out for dinner?	**Would you rather . . . or . . .**	eat Chinese or Mexican food?
Would you like to . . .	go shopping?	**Wouldn't you rather . . .**	stay home?
Wouldn't you like to . . .	go somewhere this weekend?	**Don't you think we should . . .**	save our money?
We should . . .	spend more time at the gym.		

EXERCISE 2: Preview Vocabulary

Fill in the blanks with a suggestion or alternative. More than one answer may be right for each. Use expressions from Speaking Strategy 1.

1. _____ go to Fred's party?

2. I _____ go out alone—with just you.

3. _____n't you like to go to the new romance movie instead?

4. _____ try the new restaurant around the corner.

5. Wouldn't you _____ have me cook at home?

6. _____ go shopping.

7. Don't you _____ stay home and study?

8. _____ if we go for a walk?

CULTURAL POINT

Make Suggestions Softer

Americans sometimes like to soften their speech. (See Chapter 7, "Cultural Point: Soften Your Opinion.").The verbs, *could* and *would* help to soften speech when people make suggestions, such as:

Would you help me with this [...]?
Would you lend me your [...]?
Could I borrow your [...]?
Could you show me how to [...]?

In everyday situations, women tend to use "could" and "would" more often than men. However, research shows that professional men often also use "could" and "would". And men, in general, use these "softening" expressions if they really want something.

Guess the Idiom

Let's "hang out" at the student center.

   a. Let's stick out at the student center
   b. Let's live at the student center.
   c. Let's spend our free time at the student center.

STEP 2: Listening

C O M P R E H E N S I O N

EXERCISE 3: Listen and Fill in

Listen to "Conversation: Going to Fred's Place." Check (✓) the expressions that you hear and add the verb that follows each.

   ✓ **1.** Let's _____get_____
   ____ **2.** I'd like to _____
   ____ **3.** We could _____
   ____ **4.** I'd rather _____
   ____ **5.** Diana would rather _____
   ____ **6.** Don't you think we _____
   ____ **7.** Couldn't we _____
   ____ **8.** Would you like _____
   ____ **8.** Would you like _____
   ____ **9.** Wouldn't you rather _____
   ____**10.** Would you rather _____
   ____**11.** Could I _____
   ____**12.** We should _____, don't you think?

EXERCISE 4: Listen for Reasons

Listen again to the conversation. Write one more question in the blank. Answer all of the questions and discuss your answers with a partner. Share with your class.

1. Where are Alan and Susan going to hang out?

2. Why does Susan want to bring her friend Diana?

3. Why is Susan going to drive?

4. Why are they going to Bill's Burger Place on the way to the party?

5. Add your own "why" question here: _____

EXERCISE 5: Fill in Expressions and Speakers

A. Listen again to the Conversation. Fill in the missing expressions and the speakers' names. (Hint: You may not know the names at first.)

_____ : **1.** Susan, how are you? Do you _____ at Fred's place?

_____ : **2.** Wow, that _____!

_____ : **3.** Could I _____, Diana?

__Alan__ : **4.** No _____. I'll pick _____ at 8.

_____ : **5.** _____, _____ have me drive?

_____ : **6.** Yeah, I'd _____ and _____ drive. _____ idea.

_____ : **7.** _____ we get something _____ on the way?

_____ : **8.** I'd _____ a salad, _____ Diana _____ a hamburger and fries.

_____ : **9.** _____ some burgers at Bill's Burger Place.

_____ :**10.** _____. They have salads, _____, and they're fast.

B. Read the conversation with a partner.

EXERCISE 6: Find Suggestions and Alternatives

Write some examples of suggestions and alternatives from the conversation. Compare your answers with a partner.

Alan says . . .

1. _____

2. _____

Susan says . . .

1. _____

2. _____

STEP 3: Speaking

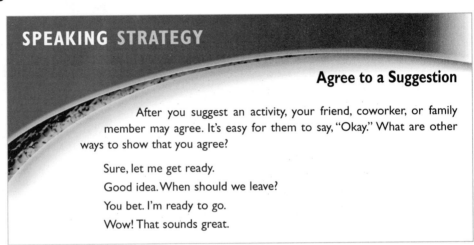

SPEAKING STRATEGY

Agree to a Suggestion

After you suggest an activity, your friend, coworker, or family member may agree. It's easy for them to say, "Okay." What are other ways to show that you agree?

Sure, let me get ready.

Good idea. When should we leave?

You bet. I'm ready to go.

Wow! That sounds great.

EXERCISE 7: Distinguish Types of Expressions

 Listen to the recording and check (✓) "Agreement" or "Alternative" for each expression.

	Agreement	Alternative
1.		
2.		
3.		
4.		
5.		
6.		

EXERCISE 8: Create a Dialogue

A. With a partner, arrange the lines to make a dialogue between Jim and Mary. There are more lines than necessary, and your conversation may differ from your classmates'conversations.

> **SITUATION:** Mary and Jim are trying to decide what to do on Friday evening. They have been dating for several months. What will they say?

Possible dialogue lines:

> I guess I'd rather see a movie with you.
>
> I heard Fred is having a party at his house. Let's go.
>
> I'd rather go to the new movie that just came out.
>
> Let's just stay home. We could barbecue a couple of steaks.
>
> Couldn't we go over to Fred's house later?
>
> Wouldn't you rather get something to eat first?
>
> Pizza wasn't what I had in mind.
>
> Good idea. Let's order some pizza to take there.

B. Read your conversation with your partner. Then, change parts and read it again.

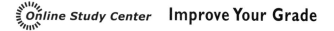 **Online Study Center**   **Improve Your Grade**

STEP 4: Stepping It Up

ANALYSIS

EXERCISE 9: Categorize the Expressions

Write **1**, **2**, or **3** in front of each sentence. Use these categories: **1** = express an opinion, **2** = make a suggestion, and **3** = give an alternative.

_____ **a.** You made a good point, but I'd rather go to the library to study.

_____ **b.** Parties are dangerous. You may not agree with me, but I don't want to go.

_____ **c.** Let's go out to a movie then. We really need to relax. How about 7 o'clock?

_____ **d.** I would rather stay home and study. I'm just wearing my old jeans.

_____ **e.** Wouldn't you like to meet my friends? They are all going to be at Jim's house.

_____ **f.** Come on, let's just go out. It will relax you. That test we took was hard.

_____ **g.** I personally believe that drinking coffee is not good for your health.

_____ **h.** Hey, I'm not talking about getting wild. Let's just have some fun.

_____ **i.** Well, don't you think *I* should drive since you're really tired?

EXERCISE 10: **Tell Your Ideas**

In the following situations, decide what suggestions and alternatives you can make. Use expressions from Speaking Strategy 1. Share your ideas.

1. Brad will have a big psychology test tomorrow. You're his friend, and you must do a big reading assignment for biology. What is your suggestion?

You: _____

2. Cindy's parents are visiting her for the weekend. She's not a very good cook. You and Lee are her best friends. What are your suggestions?

You: _____

Lee: _____

3. Dale and Jane are going out on a date Saturday night. What activities does Jane suggest? What does Dale give as an alternative?

Jane: _____

Dale: _____

4. Tom and Penny are hungry. What can Tom suggest? How does Penny respond?

Tom: _____

Penny: _____

5. Your teacher wants you to talk with 10 new strangers in English BEFORE class tomorrow. What alternative can you give? How does your teacher respond?

You: _____

Your teacher: _____

6. Your best friend suggests that you take an expensive trip together to New York City. What alternative can you give?

You: _____

7. Jim is driving the family car on a vacation. His wife Susan and his daughter need a break to go to the restroom. What can Susan suggest to her husband?

Susan: _____

8. Your friend has been calling you long-distance every weekend. You know she has a computer and e-mail. What alternative can you suggest?

You: _____

EXERCISE 11: **Create Your Own Situations**

A. Write a situation similar to those in Exercise 10.

SITUATION: _____

_____

_____

_____

B. In a group, take turns reading your situations, making suggestions, and giving alternatives. Share with your class when you finish.

EXERCISE 12: Prepare the Project

Your unit project is a role-play game that will practice expressions from the whole unit. You may want to read the project description at the end of this unit.

Create three role-play situations. These situations should be about expressing opinions, preferences, suggestions, and alternatives. You may get ideas anywhere in Unit 3. These situations will be used in a role-play game. One situation should be safe, or easy. One should be risky, or a little difficult. One should be extreme, or very difficult.

Safe (1 point)—Persuade someone to save your seat while you go to the rest-room.

Risky (5 points)—Tell one of your teachers in another class your opinion about the class. This can be a positive comment or a polite criticism.

Extreme (10 points)—After class, ask a classmate (who is not already a friend) to do something with you on the weekend. Express your preference. What activity do you want to do? Go to a movie, meet for coffee, etc.

EXERCISE 13: Evaluate Your Learning

A. Mark all the boxes that apply to your learning.

☐ I know some expressions for making suggestions.

☐ I can understand some expressions for suggesting alternatives.

☐ I know how to tell someone what I prefer to do.

☐ I know some expressions for agreeing to a suggestion.

B. Think about what was the most enjoyable part of this chapter for you. Write at least three sentences.

_____

_____

_____

Online Study Center   **Ace the Test!**

DISAGREE WITHOUT OFFENDING

Listening Focus: Problem Solving

Ask Yourself
How can you disagree without hurting someone's feelings?

STEP 1: Pre-Listening

K N O W L E D G E

EXERCISE 1: Discuss Warm-Up Questions

Ask the questions in the chart of two classmates. Write their answers in the spaces.

Questions	Names	
1. What is a favor? Who asks you to do favors for them?		
2. When people ask for a favor, what do you usually tell them?		
3. Do you often say, "Yes" or "Okay, I'll do it"? What happens if you say, "No, I can't do it"?		
4. In what situations do you say "Yes"? In what situations do you say, "No"?		

☀ *Online Study Center*   **Prepare for Class**

EXERCISE 2: Preview Vocabulary

Match the expressions to their meanings.

	Expression		Meaning
_____	**1.** a pain in the neck	**a.**	to say "no" to something
_____	**2.** to pass the time	**b.**	to persuade someone
_____	**3.** to pass up something	**c.**	It's something that you like to do.
_____	**4.** to talk someone into	**d.**	a bother; an annoyance
_____	**5.** to put a stop to	**e.**	to do what you prefer
_____	**6.** to just stand around	**f.**	to stop someone from doing something
_____	**7.** It's right up your alley.	**g.**	to keep yourself busy for a while
_____	**8.** to suit yourself	**h.**	to wait while standing up

EXERCISE 3: Unscramble the Expressions

Work with a partner to unscramble the expressions. Write them in the correct order.

1. [alley.] [right] [It's] [your] [up]

_____

2. [to] [I] [fun.] [put] [don't] [your] [want to] [a stop]

_____

3. [neck.] [pain] [a] [in the] [It's]

_____

4. [pass] [can't] [exciting.] [You] [too] [up.] [It's] [it]

_____

5. [really hard to] [around] [It is] [just stand] [something] [and wait for] [to happen.]

_____

STEP 2: Listening

COMPREHENSION

EXERCISE 4: Get the Gist

 Listen to "Conversation: Waiting in Line" and answer the questions. Use these idioms in your answers: *just stand around, put a stop to, pain in the neck, suit yourself, pass up, right up your alley, pass the time,* and *not passing up.*

1. Where are John and George? What are they doing?

   _____

2. What are John and George discussing?

   _____

3. Why doesn't George like the idea of playing the cell phone game?

   _____

4. What does John say to try to persuade him?

   _____

5. What does George prefer to do? How does he express his preference?

   _____

6. Do you think that John is happy with George's preference? What does John say to let you know his reaction? (Hint: You can use two idioms here.)

   _____

7. How does George make John feel better?

   _____

LISTENING STRATEGY

Listen for Voice Intonation

How do we know what emotion people are feeling from the sound of their voice?

"Intonation" is the answer. Intonation is change in pitch. In other words, we say words or phrases in a high or low voice.

There are different ways that a person uses pitch to show emotion:

- If someone emphasizes a word, that word may help express an opinion.
- If someone separates words and makes them low pitched, this may mean that he is angry.
- If someone's voice is high pitched, he or she might be surprised or very happy.
- If someone uses an up-and-down pitch, this shows uncertainty or nervousness.

EXERCISE 5: Listen for Emotions

 Listen to the recording and circle the emotions that the speakers express.

SITUATION 1: A speaker emphasizes certain words to express an opinion.

1. How is Mary feeling?
   - **a.** happy
   - **b.** surprised
   - **c.** very angry

SITUATION 2: A speaker separates words and says them in a low-pitched voice.

2. How is George's boss feeling?
   - **a.** sad
   - **b.** angry
   - **c.** lonely

SITUATION 3: One speaker uses different pitches. The other's voice is high-pitched.

3. How is the woman feeling?
   - **a.** calm
   - **b.** sad
   - **c.** excited

4. How is the man feeling?
   - **a.** nervous
   - **b.** sad
   - **c.** silly

STEP 3: Speaking

EXERCISE 6: Speak with Emotion

Choose an emotion for each statement. Read the statements aloud. Ask a class-mate to guess the emotion. Practice expressing different emotions.

surprised	sorry	disappointed
angry	nervous	excited and surprised
sad	happy	calm

1. What? John, I thought we had a date to go to the movies.
2. No, I didn't do it. I forgot again.
3. This is getting to be a pain in the neck. Please do it tomorrow.
4. I didn't hire you to just stand around talking to your girlfriend! Get to work!
5. Wow! What a beautiful diamond ring! Are you giving me this?
6. I couldn't pass up this opportunity to ask you . . . well, to ask you to marry me.
7. My car's not working right, can you look at it?
8. My teacher didn't like my homework. I have to do it again.
9. Congratulate me. I talked my parents into buying me a new computer.

SPEAKING STRATEGY

Express Preferences Politely

How can we politely say "No" and express our preferences?
When someone asks you to do something, how can you say "No"?
For example, imagine that Ted says to George:

George, let's stop by Ken's house on the way to the library.

Which of the following is the most polite response for George to make?

   a. I can't.
   b. No way, I don't have time.
   c. How about if we stop by there after we're done at the library?

Answer "c" is most polite because George makes a suggestion to do something else. It is also less direct than the other choices. In Chapters 7 and 8, you have been practicing ways to express your preference. As you listen to the conversation in this chapter, listen for expressions of preference.

EXERCISE 7: Express Preferences

A. There are many ways to express your preference. Read and repeat these:

I'd prefer to . . . rather than. . . .

I'd much prefer to . . . rather than. . . .

Let's . . . instead of. . . .

B. Match the beginnings and ends of the sentences.

_____ **1.** Let's go to a movie

_____ **2.** I'd much prefer to play basketball

_____ **3.** I'd much prefer to eat at home

_____ **4.** I'd prefer to take Ms. Simm's math class

_____ **5.** I'd prefer to buy the CD

   a. rather than download the music.

   b. rather than go to a restaurant.

   c. rather than Dr. Miller's history class.

   d. rather than go jogging.

   e. instead of watching a video at home.

C. Create two new sentences. Share them with your classmates.

EXERCISE 8: Disagree without Offending

Partner A starts with a suggestion. Partner B responds according to the information below. Then, change parts. For help, see Exercise 7.

Example 1:

Partner A (suggestion):   I feel like doing something fun. Let's go ice skating.

Partner B (response):   Really? But I don't know how to. I'd prefer to go bowling rather than ice skating.

Example 2:

Partner B (suggestion):   I love riding horses. I have some friends with horses. You want to come?

Partner A (response):   Let's ride bicycles instead of horses. I'm frightened of horses.

Partner A	Partner B
1. "Let's go out for pizza."	You are on a diet and don't like cheese. How can you respond to Partner A's suggestion?
2. "Would you like to go to a hip-hop concert next Saturday?"	You don't like hip-hop music. You do like classical music like Mozart.
3. "I love playing soccer. I'm on a team. Want to come watch us?"	Soccer is a boring game for you. You don't know the rules and can't follow it.
Switch parts.	
Partner A	**Partner B**
4. Unfortunately, you don't dance well. You get embarrassed easily.	"Let's go out dancing."
5. Plays are boring for you. You can't follow the dialogue well.	"Would you like to go to a play Saturday night?"
6. Chess! What a pain in the neck. It just takes too much time.	"I love playing chess. We have a chess club on campus. Want to join us?"

ANALYSIS

⠿ *Online Study Center*   **Improve Your Grade**

STEP 4: **Stepping It Up**

S Y N T H E S I S

EXERCISE 9: **Listen to Reality TV**

Watch a reality TV show. As you watch, record suggestions, alternatives, and disagreements that you hear. In the chart, check (✓) each emotion that you hear in people's voices. Add more emotions, if necessary. Copy the chart on a separate piece of paper if you need more space.

NAME OF SHOW: _____ Date: _____ Time: _____

A. Emotions that I heard:

_____ happy	_____ nervous	_____ upset	_____
_____ surprised	_____ disappointed	_____ sad	_____
_____ excited	_____ sorry	_____ angry other: _____

B. How many times did you hear these? Give a sample of each.

Suggestions	Alternatives	"No" or Other Disagreement

EXERCISE 10: **Prepare the Project**

Look again at the role-play cards from Chapter 8, Exercise 12, in a small group. Decide together if each situation really is safe, risky, or extreme. Add more cards if possible. Write or type them neatly on individual pieces of paper or cards. Ask your instructor to approve them. At the end of this unit, there are more guidelines for the project.

E
V
A
L
U
A
T
I
O
N

EXERCISE 11: **Evaluate Your Learning**

Answer the questions as you think about your learning.

1. How can I express preferences without offending others?

2. How can I express my emotions with idioms such as "It's a pain in the neck" and "It's right up my alley"?

   _____

Online Study Center   **ACE the Test!**

Online Teaching Center   **Unit Assessment**

Instructors: Print out the unit assessment. Play the appropriate assessment recording for the class.

PROJECT

Role-Play **Game**

S
Y
N
T
H
E
S
I
S

Goal

You will practice expressing your opinions, preferences, suggestions, and alternatives.

Description

You will create role-play situations, revise them, and then do them. Each situation will be given points—safe (1 point), risky (5 points), or extremely risky (10 points). Your instructor will approve the situations. You will take one or two cards every class. Do the role-plays on the cards in front of a witness outside of class. Have the witness sign your Witness Sheet. Then describe what happened to the class.

Preparation 1: Make Role-Play Cards

See Chapter 8, Exercise 12.

Preparation 2: Group Revision

See Chapter 9, Exercise 10.

Game

Every class period, take 1 or 2 cards. Then do the role-plays on the cards outside of class before the next class meeting. Have the witness write the role-play number, location, time, signature, and date. Then describe to the class what happened. Your instructor will keep track of the scores.

Feedback

What did you like about this game?

Did you have any funny experiences that you can share?

What would you do differently if you played this game again?

How do you think this game helped you improve your English?

Assessment Chart

Your instructor will use the following rubric to assess your work throughout the project.

Student Name:						
	Criteria	**0** None of the Time	**2** Some of the Time	**3** Most of the Time	**4** All of the Time	**Comments**
I.	**Made Role-Play Cards** Did each student hand in three role-plays?					
2.	**Group Revision** Did the students interact, discussing and asking questions?					
3.	**Game** Did each student try at least three role-plays? Did their description of each situation include all the necessary information?					
4.	**Respect** Did the students encourage and support each other?					
	Total Points:					

UNIT 4

BUSINESS ETHICS

Content Area:
Business

Skills You Will Learn

In this unit, you will:

Listen for definitions.

Identify reasons why something happens.

Listen for and give examples.

Identify both sides of an issue.

Listen for advice.

Ask for advice.

Give advice.

Predict a response.

Understand tag questions.

Ask for agreement.

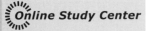
Online Study Center

http://college.hmco.com/pic/teskeone1e

93

10

ETHICS AND BIG BUSINESS

Listening Focus: Mini-Lecture

Ask Yourself
Is "right and wrong" different for businesses than for individual people?

STEP 1: Pre-Listening

KNOWLEDGE

EXERCISE 1: Discuss Warm-Up Questions

Mark the places that show your feelings about the situations. Discuss your answers with your classmates.

	Not a Problem	Not Recommended	Very Bad	Fire the Worker!
1. take pens from your workplace to use at home				
2. use work software at home without buying it				
3. tell people your company has more money than it does				
4. make long-distance personal calls at work				
5. sell a very expensive product to a customer who just needs a basic product				

Online Study Center   Prepare for Class

Guess the Idiom

My children "get into trouble" all the time.

   a. My children often do things that make me punish them.

   b. My children often have no problems.

   c. My children often go to a place called Trouble.

EXERCISE 2: Preview Vocabulary I

Listen to the recording. Guess the meaning of the underlined words. Use the information in the sentences to help you.

  I. Sam likes his <u>coworkers</u>. The people who work with him at his job get a lot of work done quickly.

    My guess: (coworker) _____

  2. Susan made a <u>high-risk</u> <u>investment</u>. She put a lot of money into the company. She could lose a lot of money, or she could make a lot of money.

    My guess: (high-risk) _____

    My guess: (investment) _____

  3. What is the right thing to do? Sometimes we make <u>unethical</u> decisions because we want to make lots of money. We are willing to make wrong or bad decisions. Some companies make the right, or <u>ethical</u>, decisions.

    My guess: (unethical) _____

    My guess: (ethical) _____

  4. Before Martin got a <u>loan</u> from the bank to buy his car, he called his <u>accountant</u>. His accountant checked Martin's situation. He agreed that Martin should borrow money from the bank.

    My guess: (loan) _____

    My guess: (accountant) _____

  5. Shirley <u>got fired</u> from her job because her <u>bosses</u> said she was late everyday. She couldn't believe she lost her job. So, she <u>took to court</u> her supervisors who made the decision. She asked the judge to punish them. However, the judge said that it was legal for her bosses to fire her.

    My guess: (got fired) _____

    My guess: (bosses) _____

    My guess: (took to court) _____

6. I have a plan for spending my money. My friends want me to share my <u>financial</u> plan with them.

    My guess: (financial) _____

7. If a <u>corporation</u> spends too much money on <u>luxury</u>, it might lose all its money. Then the company will be <u>bankrupt</u> and will not be able to buy very expensive things anymore.

    My guess: (corporation) _____

    My guess: (luxury) _____

    My guess: (bankrupt) _____

8. Harry is <u>greedy</u>. He never has enough money, so he decided to steal some cash from his company. His <u>punishment</u> was to spend 2 years in prison. Going to prison was his "payment" for doing a bad thing.

    My guess: (greedy) _____

    My guess: (punishment) _____

EXERCISE 3: Preview Vocabulary 2

Fill in the crossword puzzle.

Across

6. _____ is another word for "company."
7. never has enough money
8. When you borrow money from a bank, you get a _____.
9. "Living in _____" means you have very expensive things.
10. wrong or bad actions

Down

1. lose all your money
2. My plan for how to use money is my _____ plan.
3. a person who keeps financial records
4. Sometimes you have more than one supervisor at work.
5. You take someone to _____ and ask the judge to punish them.

STEP 2: Listening

C O M P R E H E N S I O N

EXERCISE 4: Understand WH Information

Listen to "Mini-Lecture: Business Ethics." Answer the questions.

1. What is "ethical trouble"? _____
2. Where is the large energy company that tried to make a lot of money too fast?
   _____
3. What kind of company was owned by a family that bought luxury apartments? _____
4. Who did not want to report unethical actions? _____
5. Why are employees afraid to report unethical actions? _____
   _____
6. What should a good company do? _____

LISTENING STRATEGY

Use Examples to Express Yourself

A *reason* is a fact that explains why something happened. A reason can also explain a decision or opinion.

An *example* helps us explain reasons and opinions more clearly. It paints a picture in the listener's mind. An example supports the reason or opinion. Examples often begin with:

1. For example. . . .
2. For instance. . . .
3. A good example is (*noun*). . . .
4. A good example is that (*subj. + verb*). . . .

A P P L I C A T I O N

EXERCISE 5: Listen for Reasons and Supporting Examples

Listen again to the Mini-Lecture. Fill in three reasons why businesses get into trouble. Write an example to support each reason.

Reason 1: The bosses try to grow _____

Example: _____

Reason 2: _____

Example: _____

Reason 3: _____

Example: _A company accountant saw a problem, but she said nothing._

STEP 3: Speaking

EXERCISE 6: Give an Example

Complete the opinions. (See Chapter 7 for a review of information about giving opinions.) Write some examples to support your opinions. Share them with the class. Use applause to show agreement.

> **In my opinion,** people are often not considerate. **A good example is that** a woman moved ahead of me in line at the bank.

1. **In my opinion,** unethical people should _____.
   A good example is that _____.

2. **I personally feel** education is _____.
   For example, _____.

3. **I really think** everyone should _____
   _____.

4. **I personally believe** that shopping is _____.
   _____.

5. **You may not agree with me, but I believe** _____ is wrong.
   _____.

ANALYSIS

EXERCISE 7: Define by Example

Ask your classmates for meanings of the words in the chart. Then ask them for examples. Fill in the chart with your results. Copy the chart on a separate piece of paper if you need more space.

Student A:	Do you know what luxury means?
Student B:	Yes, luxury means very expensive and very good.
Student A:	Could you give me an example of how it is used?
Student B:	Sure. I like luxury cars.

Word	Classmate's Name	Meaning	Example	Did the example help explain the meaning? Yes or No?
1. coworkers				
2. greedy				
3. unethical				
4. bankrupt				
5. corporation				
6. took to court				
7. get fired				
8. financial				

Online Study Center   Improve Your Grade

STEP 4: Stepping It Up

EXERCISE 8: Research a Business Person

A. Research a business person whom you like or admire, for example, Bill Gates, Donald Trump, Hillary Clinton, or Martha Stewart. Use magazines, newspapers, books, and the Internet to find information.

B. Use your research to answer the following questions.

RESEARCH QUESTIONS:

1. Whom are you researching?

_____

2. Where was the person born? And when? How long has the person lived?

_____

_____

3. What kind of work is the person famous for?

_____

_____

_____

4. Why did you choose this person? List two reasons and give at least one example.

Reason 1:

_____

Example:

_____

Reason 2:

_____

Example:

_____

EXERCISE 9: Practice Speaking for TOEFL® Success

Talk about a successful business person. Tell and support your opinions about why he or she is successful. You have 1 minute. Talk about only one or two main ideas. Here are some questions to guide you:

- What is his or her name?
- What is he or she famous for?
- What is his or her background?
- Why is he or she successful?

EXERCISE 10: Evaluate Your Learning

What were two things you learned in this chapter? Give an example for each.

1. I learned _____
   Example: _____
2. I learned _____
   Example: _____

E V A L U A T I O N

 *Online Study Center*   **ACE the Test!**

MAKING GOOD DECISIONS

Listening Focus: Conversation

Ask Yourself

How do you usually make decisions?
Do you list good points and bad
points for the decision?
Do you ask for advice?

STEP 1: Pre-Listening

KNOWLEDGE

EXERCISE 1: Discuss Warm-Up Questions

Discuss with a small group. Write some of your answers and share them with
your whole class.

1. Do you make good decisions by yourself?

2. Do you usually talk to someone else before you make a decision?

3. How do you know what the right decision is?

4. Can you share a difficult decision with your group? What helped you make
   the decision?

5. Is there a decision you are thinking about these days? Ask your group
   members for their opinions.

Online Study Center   Prepare for Class

EXERCISE 2: Unscramble the Expressions

Work with a partner and unscramble the expressions. Write them in the blanks. Write a sample sentence for each.

1. **Hint:** make a decision

   | your | | mind | | up | | make |

   _____ _____ _____ _____

   Sample sentence: _____

2. **Hint:** discouraged, depressed, or very sad

   | the | | down | | in | | dumps |

   _____ _____ _____ _____

   Sample sentence: _____

3. **Hint:** learned something for the first time

   | out | | found |

   _____ _____

   Sample sentence: _____

4. **Hint:** give a warning to someone that you will do a dangerous thing

   | to | | do | | something | | threaten |

   _____ _____ _____ _____

   Sample sentence: _____

5. **Hint:** look at carefully or study

   | over | | go |

   _____ _____

   Sample sentence: _____

6. **Hint:** repay for being helpful

   | do | | in | | return | | something |

   _____ _____ _____ _____

   Sample sentence: _____

7. **Hint:** I am sure

| bet | | I |

_____   _____

Sample sentence: _____

8. **Hint:** be removed from a job

| fired | | get |

_____   _____

Sample sentence: _____

EXERCISE 3: Fill in Word Forms

Complete the chart with the appropriate word forms.

	WORD FORMS			
	Noun	**Verb**	**Adjective**	**Adverb**
1.	cheer	cheer up	cheerful	cheerfully
2.	gloom	--------------		gloomily
3.	------------	determine		determinedly
4.	unhappiness	--------------	unhappy	
5.	reassurance	reassure		reassuringly
6.	doubt	doubt		doubtfully
7.	disgust	----------------	disgusted	

EXERCISE 4: Identify the Meanings

Match each adverb from the "Word Forms" chart above with its meaning.

1. brightly and happily: _____

2. in a strong, firm manner: _____

3. sadly: _____

4. in a comforting manner: _____

5. with a strong dislike: _____

6. with no pleasure: _____

7. with uncertainty: _____

EXERCISE 5: **Work with Word Forms**

Make sentences with at least five adjectives from the Word Forms Chart. Share them with a partner.

1. _____
2. _____
3. _____
4. _____
5. _____
6.   *I am determined to graduate.* _____

STEP 2: **Listening**

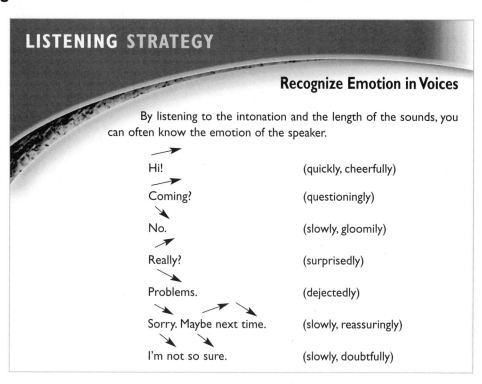

LISTENING STRATEGY

Recognize Emotion in Voices

By listening to the intonation and the length of the sounds, you can often know the emotion of the speaker.

Hi!	(quickly, cheerfully)
Coming?	(questioningly)
No.	(slowly, gloomily)
Really?	(surprisedly)
Problems.	(dejectedly)
Sorry. Maybe next time.	(slowly, reassuringly)
I'm not so sure.	(slowly, doubtfully)

EXERCISE 6: **Recognize Emotions in Intonation I**

 Listen to "Conversation: Some Friendly Advice." Listen for the emotion in the speakers' voices. Match the adverbs in the box with the speakers.

cheerfully	gloomily	unhappily	doubtfully
disgustedly	determinedly	questioningly	reassuringly

Ted	
Joe	*gloomily,*
Winnie	

EXERCISE 7: Identify Both Sides of the Issue

 A. Listen again to the Conversation. Next to the top fish bones, write three reasons that you hear *for* lying to the boss's wife. These reasons are the "pros." Next to the bottom fish bones, write three reasons that you hear *against* lying to the boss's wife. These reasons are the "cons."

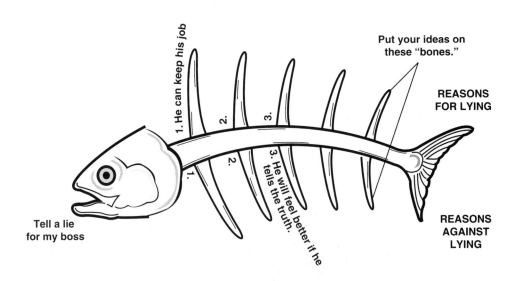

Put your ideas on these "bones."

REASONS FOR LYING

REASONS AGAINST LYING

1. He can keep his job

3. He will feel better if he tells the truth.

Tell a lie for my boss

B. Write your own ideas on the extra bones. Share them with your classmates.

EXERCISE 8: Listen for Advice

 Listen again to the Conversation. Answer the questions.

1. What advice does Winnie give? _____

_____

2. Does Winnie give more reasons for lying or against lying? _____

3. What advice does Ted give? _____

_____

4. Does Ted give more reasons for lying or against lying? _____

5. In your opinion, who gave the best advice? Why? _____

_____

STEP 3: Speaking

A P P L I C A T I O N

EXERCISE 9: Recognize Emotions in Intonation 2

Listen to the recording. You will hear "No" expressed with the various emotions in the box. Write the adverb that describes each speaker's emotion.

doubtfully	disgustedly	determinedly
gloomily	cheerfully	reassuringly

Speaker 1. _____   Speaker 2. _____

Speaker 3. _____   Speaker 4. _____

Speaker 5. _____   Speaker 6. _____

EXERCISE 10: Express Emotions through Intonation

A. Find a partner. Partner A says the word "No" with the various emotions in the box. Partner B guesses which emotion is expressed each time.

cheerfully	gloomily	doubtfully
disgustedly	determinedly	reassuringly

B. Switch parts. Partner B says the word "Really" with different emotions and Partner A guesses.

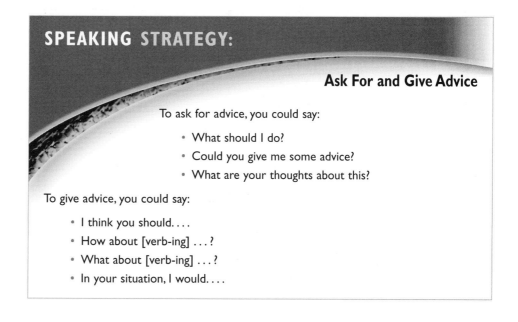

SPEAKING STRATEGY:

Ask For and Give Advice

To ask for advice, you could say:

- What should I do?
- Could you give me some advice?
- What are your thoughts about this?

To give advice, you could say:

- I think you should. . . .
- How about [verb-ing] . . . ?
- What about [verb-ing] . . . ?
- In your situation, I would. . . .

EXERCISE 11: Ask For and Give Advice

A. With a partner, read Situations 1, 2, and 3 together and take turns asking for advice and giving advice.

SITUATION 1:

You were just promoted to a management job. Your boss calls you into her office and questions you about your former coworkers (now your *employees*). She makes you feel like you have to tell her gossip about former coworkers.

Ask for advice: _What_ _____ **?**

Give advice: _I think you should_ _____ **.**

SITUATION 2:

You are the manager of a small department. Most of your staff is fine, but one employee is not able to do all her work. She is very excited at work and she makes everyone happy. Another employee is very good at his work, but his coworkers and the customers do not like him. He is gloomy most of the time. Your boss just told you to fire someone.

Ask for advice: _____

Give advice: _____

SITUATION 3:

Your secretary at work helped you finish your big project last week. She wants to leave work early today. The problem is that she did not tell you soon enough. You want to do something for her in return, but she hasn't finished her accounting report.

Ask for advice: _____

Give advice: _____

B. By yourself, write about a difficult situation from your own experience. Read it to your partner and ask for advice. Your partner will give you advice.

_____

_____

_____

Ask your partner for advice: _____

My partner's advice is: _____

≋Online Study Center **Improve Your Grade**

STEP 4: Stepping It Up

SYNTHESIS

EXERCISE 12: Interview Someone about a Job

A. Prepare to interview someone who works at a job that you are interested in. Write some:

- introductory, or small-talk, questions,
- general questions about the job,
- questions about the pros and cons of the job.

Sample questions:

1. How are you today?

2. Thank you for agreeing to this interview. How long have you worked here?

3. What is your usual work schedule?

4. *(Use your imagination and write about five more questions. Use a separate piece of paper.)*

B. Interview the person and take notes. At the end of the interview, ask for advice about your (future) career choice.

C. In a small group, share the information that you learned in the interview.

EXERCISE 13: **Prepare the Project**

Your unit project is to create a corporation. In a short presentation to your class, you will give reasons why this corporation should exist and examples of how it will serve others. Prepare for this project by forming a partnership with one other class member.

- Brainstorm and create a corporation.
- Think about what kind of business will succeed and not go bankrupt.
- Keep your notes because you will continue the project in Chapter 12.

EXERCISE 14: **Evaluate Your Learning**

Mark each item as either True or False.

True	False		
		1.	I discovered and learned some new adverbs.
		2.	I identified the emotion of a speaker by listening for intonation.
		3.	I asked for advice.
		4.	I got some new information about a job that I'm interested in.
		5.	I discovered some pros and cons about that job.

Online Study Center   **ACE the Test!**

BUSINESS DILEMMAS

Listening Focus: Problem Solving

Ask Yourself
How do you feel about people who take work supplies to use at home?

STEP 1: Pre-Listening

KNOWLEDGE

EXERCISE 1: Discuss Warm-Up Questions

Discuss with a group. Write some of your answers and share them with your class.

1. What is the meaning of the word "honesty"?

2. Is it easy to find people who break the rules a little? Or a lot?

3. Do you share *everything* that happens at work with your boss?

4. Are there business people or coworkers that you admire? Who are they? Why do you admire them?

5. Do you think it's easy to be honest in your everyday life?

Online Study Center   **Prepare for Class**

EXERCISE 2: Preview Vocabulary

A. Match the following expressions to their meanings.

_____	**1.** What's up?	**a.** think of a lot of new ideas
_____	**2.** brainstorm ideas	**b.** an important matter
_____	**3.** formulate	**c.** in fact; actually
_____	**4.** jealous [of someone]	**d.** recognize [a person's] work
_____	**5.** give [someone] credit	**e.** have a positive effect
_____	**6.** popped into my head	**f.** should
_____	**7.** had better	**g.** What's going on?
_____	**8.** a big deal	**h.** carefully plan
_____	**9.** make a good impression	**i.** suddenly thought of something
_____	**10.** dilemma	**j.** problem with a choice of solutions
_____	**11.** as a matter of fact	**k.** envious [of someone]

B. Fill in the blanks with 10 of the expressions from Part A.

1. _____, Henry? You look like you have a big _____.

2. Are you making _____ out of this?

3. I like to _____ before I _____ a response.

4. Are you _____ of Henry's creative ideas?

5. You _____ give Henry_____ for his ideas.

6. Henry likes to _____, especially when he meets new customers.

7. That idea just _____. I guess I'm lucky.

EXERCISE 3: Fill in the Antonyms

Fill in the antonyms (opposites) for the expressions. Compare with your class-mates when you are done.

EXPRESSION:	**ANTONYM**
1. hire:	_____
2. lend:	_____
3. honesty:	_____
4. fact:	_____
5. bad impression:	_____
6. no big deal:	_____
7. never give anyone credit:	_____

STEP 2: Listening

C
O
M
P
R
E
H
E
N
S
I
O
N

EXERCISE 4: Listen for Details 1

Listen to "Problem Solving 1: The Office Thief." With a partner, answer the questions.

1. Who are the two speakers? _____

2. What is their relationship? _____

3. How do you know? What words are the clues? _____
_____

EXERCISE 5: Understand the New Expressions 1

Listen again to Problem Solving 1. Fill in the missing expressions.

1. Hey, Jim. Could I talk to you for a minute after the meeting? Sure, Bob, _____?

2. I'm really glad we _____ her.

3. She listens to me, and she listens to Julie. We _____ once in a while.

4. Well, those ideas come out of Mary's mouth before Julie and I have a chance to completely _____ them.

5. You aren't _____ our new star, are you?

6. She never _____ credit.

EXERCISE 6: **Predict Other People's Responses**

In a small group, discuss and write answers to the questions about Problem Solving 1. Share them with your class.

1. What do you think Jim, the boss, will do about this situation?

_____

2. What do you think will happen to Bob's job? Julie's job? Mary's job?

_____

3. In your opinion, do you think Bob is correct in telling Jim about Mary? Would you discuss a similar problem with your boss? Would you be willing to talk about this kind of problem?

_____

_____

EXERCISE 7: **Listen for Details 2**

Listen to "Problem Solving 2: Telling the Office Thief." With a partner, answer the questions.

1. What is the situation? _____

2. Who is involved? _____

3. How do you know? What words are the clues? _____

_____

EXERCISE 8: Understand the New Expressions 2

Listen again to Problem Solving 2. Fill in the missing expressions.

1. Well, as a _____ it is my idea.

2. It just _____ yesterday.

3. They weren't sure about the details, but they thought they _____ _____ let me know their idea before you did.

4. I don't know what to say. I wanted to _____ in this job.

5. I didn't think that if I _____ a couple of ideas that it would be such _____ .

LISTENING STRATEGY

Understand Tag Questions

A tag question is a short question that is added to the end of a statement. This type of question is usually formulated by using the same verb as in the sentence. However, if the main verb is affirmative, then the tag question is negative, or vice versa.

Tag questions ask for agreement from the other person(s) in the conversation. Tag questions use alternate falling and rising intonations at the end. The intonation depends on whether the question is negative (falling) or affirmative (rising).

You are from Germany, aren't you?

OR

You aren't from Chicago, are you?

EXERCISE 9: Understand Tag Questions

Listen again to Problem Solving 1 and 2. Fill in the tag questions that you hear.

1. Mary? She's doing great, _____ ?

2. She has some super ideas, _____ ?

3. You aren't jealous of our new star, _____ ?

4. That was your idea, _____ ?

5. This isn't the first time, _____ ?

6. Mary, you didn't borrow their ideas, _____ ?

STEP 3: Speaking

SPEAKING STRATEGY

Ask for Agreement with Tag Questions

Using tag questions to ask for agreement is quite common in English. Instead of matching a tag question to the verb in the main part of the sentence, we can add other kinds of tag questions, such as:

That was your idea, right?

She's doing great, don't you think?

Bob has super ideas, don't you agree?

EXERCISE 10: Ask for Agreement

Fill in the tag questions. Use the forms from the two strategy boxes. With a partner, take turns asking and answering them.

1. We never get out of our meetings on time, _____?

2. Our homework isn't really very hard, _____?

3. You didn't borrow my pencil, _____?

4. He's a really good instructor, _____?

5. This story didn't have a very good ending, _____?

6. My boss is really a nice guy, _____?

7. Our instructor has some super ideas, _____?

8. Watching television every day is a waste of time, _____?

9. Getting a promotion at work is pretty hard to do, _____?

10. Someone who steals ideas without giving credit is dishonest, _____?

EXERCISE 11: Predict a Response

A. With a partner, decide how Jim (the boss) and Mary will respond to the situation. Write your ideas below.

Jim _____

_____

Mary _____

_____

 B. Listen to "Problem Solving 3: The Office Thief Conclusion." Were your predictions in Part A correct?   Yes _____   No _____

EXERCISE 12: **Respond to Dishonesty**

 Listen to the recording for each situation. In a small group, create a short dialogue or written response. Share your responses with your class.

SITUATION 1: Money Missing from the Cash Receipts

RESPONSE: What should the manager (or the owner) of the restaurant do?

_____

_____

_____

_____

_____

_____

SITUATION 2: A Small Paycheck

RESPONSE: What should the first cashier do about his small paycheck?

_____

_____

_____

_____

_____

_____

Online Study Center   **Improve Your Grade**

STEP 4: **Stepping It Up**

EXERCISE 13: **Survey People at Work**

Give this survey to at least five people who have (or had) a job. Your respondents should not write their names on their papers. Organize the results and share them with your classmates.

1. Have you ever taken anything from a business that you worked at?

2. If yes, what was it? And what was the value of the thing that you took?

3. Do you feel sorry that you took something? Why or why not?

4. If you owned a business, would you be worried about employee dishonesty?

Exercise 14: Prepare the Project

You formed a partnership and created a corporation in Chapter 11. Now you need to plan out your presentation: At the end of this unit, there are more guidelines for the project.

- describe your business
- give reasons why this corporation should exist
- provide examples of how it will serve others
- at the end of your presentation, ask your classmates for advice

Remember to assign responsibilities and set deadlines to complete this part of the project.

Exercise 15: Evaluate Your Learning

Answer the questions as you think about your learning.

1. Can I make tag questions? Give an example.

    _____?

2. Can I talk about problems at work? Give an example.

    _____?

3. What new information did I learn about other people's honesty (and dishonesty) at work?

    _____?

Online Study Center   ACE the Test!

Online Teaching Center   Unit Assessment

Instructors: Print out the unit assessment. Play the appropriate assessment recording for the class.

UNIT 4

PROJECT

Go Bankrupt or Succeed?

SYNTHESIS

Goal

You will practice giving reasons, providing examples, asking for advice, giving advice, and predicting the future.

Description

Students, in pairs, create a corporation. Classmates listen to each group's description of their corporation. The whole class gives the group advice about the success or failure of the corporation and predicts what will happen to it.

Preparation 1: Create a Corporation

See Chapter 11, Exercise 13.

Preparation 2: Plan the Presentation

See Chapter 12, Exercise 14.

Presentation

PART A: Your group will have 5 minutes to present. These items should be included in your presentation:

- describe your corporation
- give reasons why this corporation should exist
- provide examples of how it will serve others
- end with a request for advice from your classmates

Remember to assign responsibilities so that both of you speak during the presentation. Develop a timeline so that you do not talk longer than 5 minutes.

PART B: Class members listen to each presentation and give their opinions. Will this corporation be able to avoid financial trouble? Predict the success of this corporation in 2 years' time.

Feedback

Evaluate your abilities to do the goals for the project. Discuss the following questions:

1. Did you have any funny experiences that you can share?
2. Did you think that any group did a great presentation? What did they do that you liked?
3. How do you think this project helped you improve your English?

Assessment Chart

Your instructor will use the following rubric to assess your work throughout the project.

GROUP MEMBERS:

Criteria	0 None of the Time	2 Some of the Time	3 Most of the Time	4 All of the Time	Comments
1. Created a corporation Do you think this group was creative?					
2. Presentation Did they both talk a lot? Did they make their ideas clear and convincing to the class?					
3. Feedback Did other students like their ideas and presentation?					
4. Respect Did these two students encourage and support each other?					
Total Points:					

UNIT
5

HEALTH CONCERNS

Content Area:
Nursing and Health

Skills You Will Learn

In this unit, you will:

Take notes on descriptions in a mini-lecture.

Choose the best summary statement about a lecture.

Use vocabulary about health.

Take notes from the Internet.

Retell and use vocabulary that is different from the original.

Understand and identify complaints as sharp or soft.

Listen to and understand a long story.

Tell a story.

Distinguish appropriate and inappropriate comments.

Express sympathy, encouragement, and offer to help.

Online Study Center

http://college.hmco.com/pic/teskeone1e

WHAT IS CANCER?

Listening Focus: Mini-Lecture

Ask Yourself

Why is it important to take notes in a lecture?

STEP 1: Pre-Listening

KNOWLEDGE

EXERCISE 1: Discuss Warm-Up Questions

Read and discuss these questions with a partner or small group.

1. Have you ever been in the hospital? Describe the experience.

2. How long do people stay in the hospital countries you are familiar with?

3. What do you do for someone who is sick or in the hospital?

4. When you hear the word "cancer," what do you think about?

5. Do you know someone who has cancer?

6. Do you know someone who has survived cancer?

7. What are some ways to support someone with cancer?

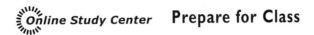 **Prepare for Class**

EXERCISE 2: Preview Vocabulary 1

Listen to the meanings and fill in the chart with your instructor. Copy the chart on a separate piece of paper if you need more space.

Nouns	Meanings	Verbs	Meanings
1. cell	a very small building-block of the body	8. spread	
2. tumor		9. vomit	to get rid of the contents of the stomach by the mouth
3. patient			
4. symptom			
5. treatment			
6. urine	A yellow fluid that contains body waste		
7. blood			

EXERCISE 3: Preview Vocabulary 2

 Listen to the recording for these antonyms. Fill in the missing information.

Adjectives	Meanings	Adjectives	Meanings
1. normal	regular	4. abnormal	not normal or _____
2. benign	_____	5. malignant	more dangerous
3. harmless	causing no injury	6. dangerous	may _____

STEP 2: Listening

**C
O
M
P
R
E
H
E
N
S
I
O
N**

EXERCISE 4: Take Notes on Descriptions

Listen to "Mini-Lecture 1: What is Cancer?" Write the phrases that describe each type of tumor.

I.   Benign (or) __harmless_____

    I.I They are _____.

    I.2 These tumors often don't need _____.

II. Malignant tumors

    2.1 They are _____ and can _____.

    2.2 They _____ into other parts of the body.

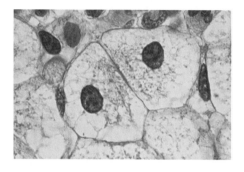

EXERCISE 5: Reproduce the Message

Listen to Mini-Lecture 1 again. Fill in the missing words in the third paragraph of the lecture.

Cancer starts at the _____ part of the body, the _____. Health cells grow and _____ as the body needs them. With cancer, the control signals in a normal cell _____ go wrong. In other words, _____ becomes _____. Then, the abnormal cell _____ dividing and _____. This big growth _____ is called a lump, or _____.

EXERCISE 6: Choose the Best Summary Statement

Check (✔) the statements that summarize well the ideas in Mini-Lecture 1. (Hint: Five are good summary statements.)

_____ **a.** There is more than one type of cancer.

_____ **b.** Many people will have cancer or know someone with cancer during their lives.

_____ **c.** Very few people die from cancer—only about 500 per year.

_____ **d.** Cancer is formed by abnormal cells.

_____ **e.** Normal cells grow quickly and divide quickly, which makes a tumor.

_____ **f.** Benign tumors often don't need treatment. They are not dangerous.

_____ **g.** Malignant tumors are not harmful.

_____ **h.** Some people get cancer because they do things like smoking, eating no vegetables, and sitting in the sun every day.

EXERCISE 7: Identify the Details

 Listen to "Mini-Lecture 2: Giving Support." Mark the following items True or False.

_____ **1.** Family and friends always know exactly what to do when they learn that someone has cancer.

_____ **2.** You may help by listening and encouraging the cancer patient to talk.

_____ **3.** Your relationship with the cancer patient may change.

_____ **4.** Help probably includes getting the person with cancer a new job in a new city.

_____ **5.** Visiting a person who has cancer is not a good idea.

_____ **6.** Seeing the person regularly and doing everyday jobs may be very helpful.

_____ **7.** Caregivers need to forget about themselves and only help the patient.

_____ **8.** Family and friends can not become caregivers because they do not work in a hospital.

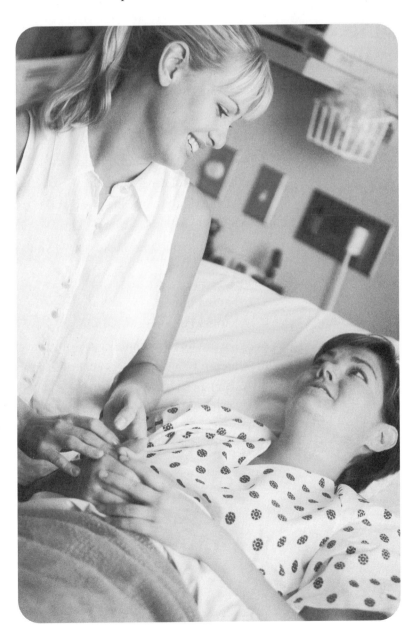

EXERCISE 8: Choose the Concluding Idea

Choose the best statement below to end Mini-Lecture 2.

a. In conclusion, be sure to express your sympathy and encouragement, not only to the patient but also to the family and to the patient's caregiver.

b. In conclusion, relatives should stay away from the person with cancer because they do not want to make trouble or cause problems.

c. In conclusion, small thoughtful actions, such as listening to the patient talk, offering help, and keeping yourself healthy, are helpful to a person with this serious disease.

d. To conclude, the best way to help patients is to bring them flowers and talk with them in the hospital.

e. In the end, you should support the patient and his family with kind words and nice thoughts.

STEP 3: Speaking

EXERCISE 9: Discuss Mini-Lecture Content

A. With a partner, take turns asking each other the questions about Mini-Lectures 1 and 2.

PARTNER A

1. According to the Mini-Lecture, how common is cancer?

3. What types of cancers are there?

5. What kind of tumor can spread and is dangerous?

7. What is an example of something you can do for a friend who has cancer?

9. Why is it important to take care of yourself too?

PARTNER B

2. What is a tumor?

4. What kind of tumor is harmless?

6. What are three common causes for cancer?

8. Who can be a caregiver? What does a caregiver do?

10. If you live far away from a patient, what support can you give? If you live close by, how can you help?

B. Discuss your answers with the class.

 Online Study Center   **Improve Your Grade**

STEP 4: Stepping It Up

EXERCISE 10: Take Notes about Cancer

A. Make a group of four. Each person choose two types of cancer from the chart to research. Do research in a library or on the Internet on the types of cancer that are listed in the chart, or add your own. (Hint: There is a lot of information. Focus on answering the questions. Use some of the new vocabulary.)

B. With your group, use the results of your research to fill in the information in the chart.

Type of Cancer	Who usually gets it?	How many people get it?	What are the symptoms?
Stomach			
Lymphoma – Non-Hodgkin's			
Breast			
Skin			
Prostate			
Lung			
Wilms' tumor			
Leukemia			

S Y N T H E S I S

EXERCISE 11: Practice Speaking for TOEFL® Success

Talk about what cancer is and how to support someone with an illness. You have 2 minutes or less. Use Exercises 9 and 10 to help you prepare. Here are some questions to guide you:

How does cancer start? What are two different kinds of tumors?

What are three ways to support someone with cancer?

Describe a specific type of cancer. Who usually gets it? What are the symptoms?

Would you recommend someone learn more about cancer? Where can they get more information?

E V A L U A T I O N

EXERCISE 12: Evaluate Your Learning

A. Mark all of the boxes that apply to your learning in this chapter.

☐ **1.** I learned some new vocabulary about the body and cancer.

☐ **2.** I can choose the best summary statement about a mini-lecture.

☐ **3.** I can take notes on new information in a mini-lecture.

☐ **4.** I am more comfortable talking about the content of a mini-lecture than I was before.

☐ **5.** I am more comfortable taking notes from the Internet.

B. Choose one of the items you checked. Write at least three sentences about what you learned.

_____

_____

_____

_____

_____

Online Study Center   **ACE the Test!**

SERIOUS ILLNESS

Listening Focus: Conversation

Ask Yourself
How do you express sympathy and encouragement?

STEP 1: Pre-Listening

K
N
O
W
L
E
D
G
E

EXERCISE 1: Discuss Warm-Up Questions

A. Interview two people. Ask them these two questions.

1. What do you usually complain about?

Person 1: _____

Person 2: _____

2. Have you ever been in the hospital? If so, can I ask what kind of problem you had?

Person 1: _____

Person 2: _____

B. With a partner, discuss these questions after you finish the interviews.

   I. You interviewed Person 1 and 2. What kind of complaints do they usually make?

   2. Have Person 1 and 2 ever been in the hospital?

   3. In other countries, what do friends and relatives generally do when someone is sick in the hospital? What do they say to the person who is sick?

   4. Tell about a time when you encouraged a family member or a friend.

Online Study Center   **Prepare for Class**

EXERCISE 2: Preview Vocabulary I

Match the expressions to their meanings.

_____ **I.** get your mind off [the pain]

_____ **2.** I can't stand [verb-*ing*]

_____ **3.** heal

_____ **4.** recover

_____ **5.** Band-Aid™

_____ **6.** bandage

_____ **7.** surgery

_____ **8.** pill

_____ **9.** prescribe

_____ **10.** prescription

_____ **II.** medication

_____ **12.** ankle

_____ **13.** throat

_____ **14.** hassle

a. passage from the back of the mouth to the stomach or lungs

b. get better

c. a piece of material that is stuck to the skin to cover cuts

d. white cloth used to protect an injury

e. written note from a doctor to a drugstore about medicine for a patient

f. officially say what treatment or medicine is needed for a sick person

g. become better after an illness

h. stop thinking about [something]

i. something that is annoying or difficult

j. joint between the foot and the leg

k. I really don't like [verb-*ing*]

l. medical treatment that requires a surgeon to cut open the body

m. medicine

n. small, solid piece of medicine

 Guess the Idiom

My feet are "killing me."

   a. My feet are tired of walking.

   b. My feet are really hurting me.

   c. My feet are causing me to die.

EXERCISE 3: Preview Vocabulary 2

Answer these questions using the words from Exercise 2.

1. What do you get from a doctor to take to the drugstore for specific medicine?
2. If your friend cut his finger, what would you recommend?
3. Let's say your friend cut his hand fairly deeply. What would you recommend?
4. Is there a medication that you like to use to help heal a sore throat?
5. Is there a type of medication that you can't stand?
6. What can you recommend for someone to take if they say, "The pain is killing me"?
7. After knee surgery, how much time do you think it takes to recover?
8. Do you think that visiting a doctor several times a month is a hassle?

STEP 2: Listening

COMPREHENSION

LISTENING STRATEGY

Listen to Complaints

When someone is sick, it is important to listen. The other person may need to complain. Sometimes you may hear complaints that are sharp and direct. At other times, you may hear complaints that are soft and indirect.

There are different expressions for each type of complaint.

Sharp Complaints	Examples
I really don't like . . .	eating hospital food.
I hate . . .	waiting so long to see the doctor.
What I can't stand is [verb-*ing*] . . .	getting up so early in the morning.
I can't stand [verb-*ing*] . . .	sitting in bed so long.
It really bothers me that . . .	I can eat hardly anything yet.

Soft Complaints	Examples
I don't care for . . .	the nurse who brings my lunch.
I don't think that . . .	the medicine is helping me.
It doesn't seem fair that . . .	I can't go back to school yet.

EXERCISE 4: Identify Complaints as Sharp or Soft

A. Listen to the recording, and in each pair, choose (✓) the complaint that you hear.

1.	_____ **A.** Really, I just don't think I can take another pill.
	_____ **B.** Really, it bothers me that I have to take another pill.
2.	_____ **A.** I hate staying in bed all day. It's boring.
	_____ **B.** I don't care for staying in bed all day. It's boring.
3.	_____ **A.** It doesn't seem fair that I have to buy such expensive medicine.
	_____ **B.** I really don't like buying such expensive medicine.
4.	_____ **A.** What I can't stand is seeing the doctor every other day.
	_____ **B.** I don't care for seeing the doctor every other day.

B. In each pair, circle the complaint that sounds softer and more polite.

EXERCISE 5: Link Situations and Complaints

A. Listen to the recording for each complaint and match it to one of the situations.
B. Work with a partner. Read four situations to your partner. Your partner answers with an appropriate complaint. Then switch.

SITUATIONS

1. Your friend has a headache. He says . . . _____d_____

2. Your grandfather has a backache. He says . . . _____

3. A man is picking up a prescription at the drugstore. He says . . . _____

4. You have to get a medical exam this month and do not have enough money. You say . . . _____

5. Your brother hurt his ankle while he was playing soccer. He has to get an X-ray at the hospital. Your mother says . . . _____

6. Your aunt has lost some of her hair because she is having cancer treatments. She says . . . _____

7. A friend of yours just had surgery on his right knee. He can't drive for six weeks and needs to get to work and to school. He says . . . _____

8. Your doctor prescribed some bad-tasting medicine for you to take. You say . . . _____

EXERCISE 6: Listen for Comments

 Read the situation. Listen to "Conversation: Visiting Aunt Susie." Answer the questions below.

SITUATION: Lilly's mother called her. She told Lilly that her aunt, Susie, was very ill and in the nearby hospital. Aunt Susie is Lilly's favorite aunt. So Lilly called the hospital to find out the visiting hours, and then she went to visit. On the way to the hospital, Lilly stopped and bought some fresh flowers in bright colors, like yellow and pink. At the hospital, Lilly checked in at the visitor's desk and found out Aunt Susie's room number. Then she went to her room.

1. When did Aunt Susie have surgery?
2. What kind of cancer does Aunt Susie have?
3. Why is Aunt Susie worried?
4. Tell a complaint that Aunt Susie has.
5. How does Lilly respond to this complaint?
6. What present did Lilly bring her aunt?
7. Why does Aunt Susie like the present?

EXERCISE 7: **Listen and Identify Complaints**

 A. Listen again to the Conversation. Write the three examples of complaints.

Complaints:

1. _____
2. _____
3. _____

B. Write three other complaints that Aunt Susie could have said.

4. _____
5. _____
6. _____

STEP 3: **Speaking**

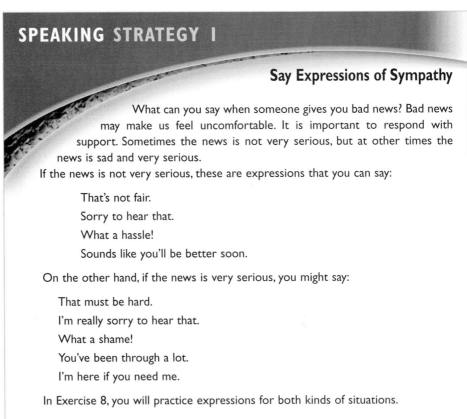

SPEAKING STRATEGY 1

Say Expressions of Sympathy

What can you say when someone gives you bad news? Bad news may make us feel uncomfortable. It is important to respond with support. Sometimes the news is not very serious, but at other times the news is sad and very serious.

If the news is not very serious, these are expressions that you can say:

That's not fair.

Sorry to hear that.

What a hassle!

Sounds like you'll be better soon.

On the other hand, if the news is very serious, you might say:

That must be hard.

I'm really sorry to hear that.

What a shame!

You've been through a lot.

I'm here if you need me.

In Exercise 8, you will practice expressions for both kinds of situations.

A P P L I C A T I O N

EXERCISE 8: Categorize Responses of Sympathy

Decide if the expressions of sympathy in the list are responses to very serious news or less serious news. Write them in the chart below, or copy the chart on a separate piece of paper if you need more space.

- That's awful!
- It's really hard to believe.
- What a hassle.
- That must be difficult.
- Sorry to hear that.
- That's not so bad. You should recover soon.

- That's not fair.
- What a shame!
- I'm really sorry to hear that.
- Oh no! Are you feeling okay?
- It sounds like you'll be better soon.
- You've been through a lot.

RESPONSES OF SYMPATHY	
Very Serious or Sad News	**Less Serious News**
	That's not fair.

EXERCISE 9: Respond with Sympathy

Listen to the recording for statements of bad news. For each, write a response in the chart and check (✓) "Very Serious" or "Less Serious." Share with your classmates.

	Response of Sympathy	Very Serious	Less Serious
I.			
2.			
3.			
4.			
5.			
6			
7.			

SPEAKING STRATEGY 2

Say Words of Encouragement

In the conversation between Lilly and Aunt Susie, Lilly said these expressions to encourage her aunt:

"I am sure that the doctor will come soon."

"It will get your mind off of the pain."

It depends on the situation, but there are other possible expressions to encourage others. The expressions in the chart are grouped according to their situations.

Show Enthusiasm due to Success	Continue on the Same Course	Continue Even Though It Is Difficult
Way to go!	Keep working on it.	I am sure that …
Good job!	You are getting there.	Try to keep your mind off of the pain.
Fantastic!	It looks like it is coming along.	Take it step by step.
I knew you could do it.	Keep going and don't give up.	Just go day by day.

EXERCISE 10: Offer Encouragement

With a partner, read and respond to these situations.

1. The doctor told me that I'm doing much better.

    Response: _____

2. I need to get more exercise every day, but I still hurt.

    Response: _____

3. I have to take all these pills, change my diet, and go to the doctor every week. It's too much to remember!

    Response: _____

4. My surgery was painful, but I am healing and getting stronger.

    Response: _____

5. My doctor told me to lose 20 pounds. I already lost 2 pounds.

    Response: _____

6. My headaches seem to be getting worse. But the doctor says that I'm taking enough medication.

    Response: _____

SPEAKING STRATEGY 3

Give Neutral Responses to Complaints

When you talk to someone who is complaining, it is a good idea to respond without agreement or disagreement. The other person may be emotional, but don't become emotional yourself. In other words, stay calm by using neutral expressions like these:

That's understandable.

I know what you mean.

How does that make you feel?

Is there more to the story?

Neutral expressions show that you are listening and that you understand.

In Exercise 11, you will practice a variety of ways to respond to complaints that show that you are calm and that you understand.

EXERCISE 11: Respond Neutrally

Match each neutral response to a complaint. (Hint: Some variation in answers is okay.)

_____ **1.** Oh, I see.

_____ **2.** I know what you mean.

_____ **3.** I can understand that.

_____ **4.** How does that make you feel?

_____ **5.** Is there any other problem?

_____ **6.** Is there more to the story?

_____ **7.** Why do you think this happened?

_____ **8.** That's understandable.

a. Today the doctor said the treatment is not working.

b. I don't care for the pain in my foot.

c. My throat hurts. My back aches. And my stomach is upset.

d. I can't stand this. It's never happened before. Why does everything happen to me?

e. . . . and then he was rushed to hospital.

f. My doctor told me to take better care of myself.

g. I hate that I feel so very tired these days.

h. Sometimes I just don't want to take so many pills.

EXERCISE 12: List Situations for Neutral Responses

Make a list of jobs where workers should use neutral responses. Compare lists with your classmates.

_____

_____

emergency-response workers _____

_____

_____

EXERCISE 13: Respond to Complaints in Different Ways

Copy the chart on a separate piece of paper. In a group of three, listen to the recording for some statements of complaint. For each complaint, the first person responds with sympathy. The second person responds with encouragement. The third person gives a neutral response. Fill in the chart as you go.

Complaint	Partner 1: Expression of Sympathy	Partner 2: Encouragement	Partner 3: Neutral Response
1. Backache			
2. Knee surgery			
3. Cancer treatment			
4. Tests at the hospital			
5. Car accident and injury			

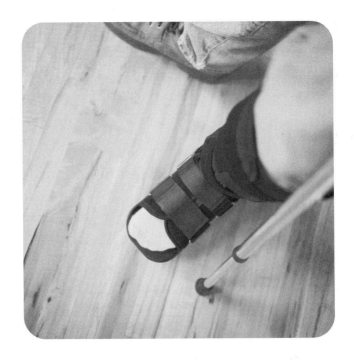

Online Study Center   **Improve Your Grade**

STEP 4: Stepping It Up

EXERCISE 14: Research Customers' Complaints

A. With a partner, list the names of some stores or service organizations that you could visit in order to do research on customer complaints.

B. With your partner or alone, go to the places on your list, and ask the clerks about customer complaints. Copy the chart below on a separate piece of paper and fill it in with the results of your research.

Store	Area Where Clerk Works	Customers' Complaints
Wally's Shoe Store	Ladies shoes	I don't care for this style.

C. Share your results with your class. Discuss how each clerk could respond to the complaints that you collected.

EXERCISE 15: Prepare the Project

The project for this unit is to interview senior citizens outside of class. There may be a senior center in the community where your class can go. However, if one is not available, each pair or group will find a retired senior citizen in the community to interview.

A. Find out about senior centers or retirement centers that you could visit. Divide into groups of two or three to research. The telephone book or Internet may have information on centers in your community. You may research under Senior Citizen Center, Senior Care Facilities, nursing home, retirement community, or others your teacher suggests.

B. Bring to class a list of at least two senior centers in your city or retired senior citizens you could interview. Include the addresses and phone numbers also.

1. _____

_____

2. _____

_____

C. Decide as a class which ones to contact. If a senior center is not available, each pair or group will find a retired senior citizen in the community to interview.

E
V
A
L
U
A
T
I
O
N

EXERCISE 16: Evaluate Your Learning

Answer the questions as you reflect on your learning.

1. Are you now able to understand complaints about health? _____

2. In what situation(s) do you usually use sympathetic responses? _____
    _____

3. What two expressions of encouragement do you feel comfortable using now?
    _____

4. When would you use a neutral response to a complaint? _____
    _____

Online Study Center   **ACE the Test!**

CHAPTER
15

A SERIES OF DILEMMAS

Listening Focus: Problem Solving

Ask Yourself
If you were really sick, how would you tell your family and friends? What could you say? How could they help you?

STEP 1: Pre-Listening

K N O W L E D G E

EXERCISE 1: Discuss Warm-Up Questions

With a partner, discuss these questions.

1. Is it easy or hard for you to share sad news? Why?
2. Tell about a time when you heard some sad news. What was the news? How did you respond?
3. When you are in a sad situation, are you usually strong?
4. Or, in sad situations, do you usually depend on other people for support?
5. Where do you find support in a sad situation?
6. Can you share how someone supported you in a sad situation?

Online Study Center   **Prepare for Class**

EXERCISE 2: Preview Vocabulary

A. Discuss these words and phrases: *sweat, chills, daycare, lymphoma, react, benefit, upset, frustrated, surgery, chemotherapy, hug, threaten, protective, insurance, medical, depressed, fever, delighted, fatigue.*

B. Write them in the chart beside their meanings. Check (✓) if they have a positive, negative, or neutral idea.

Word/Phrase	Meaning	Positive	Negative	Neutral
1.	to give off a salty liquid through the skin			
2.	a body temperature that is higher than normal			
3.	day time care for children of preschool age			
4.	a feeling of coldness		✓	
5.	a type of cancer that attacks the lymph nodes			
6.	to act in response to something			✓
7.	something that is of help or an advantage	✓		
8.	worried or unhappy because something bad happened			
9.	caused feelings of discouragement or confusion			
10.	very sad, low in spirits		✓	
11.	to hold someone closely			
12.	to be a source of danger to somebody		✓	
13.	greatly pleased			
14.	serving to protect	✓		
15.	weariness and exhaustion resulting from hard work or great effort			
16.	the business of guaranteeing to pay for specified losses in the future			
17.	the treatment of cancer by chemicals that have a negative effect on malignant cells			
18.	procedure on the body to cut body tissues and remove, repair, or replace organs			✓
19.	relating to the practice of medicine			

Guess the Idiom

We've had our "ups and downs."

    a. We have driven back and forth.

    b. We are not sure in which direction to go.

    c. We have had good times and bad times.

STEP 2: Listening

EXERCISE 3: Listen, Predict, and Understand a Long Story

 Listen to "Melissa's Story." It has three parts. In small groups, discuss the questions when the recording tells you to.

MELISSA'S STORY PART 1

  1. What should Melissa probably do now?

  2. How will Melissa react to this news?

  3. What will Melissa's husband, Frank, say about her news?

  4. Why is Frank so upset?

  5. What could Melissa say to Frank?

MELISSA'S STORY PART 2

  6. Will Melissa tell her parents her news while Justin is listening?

  7. How will Melissa's mother react to the news? In other words, what will she do?

  8. How will Melissa's father react to the news?

  9. What will Melissa ask her parents about Justin?

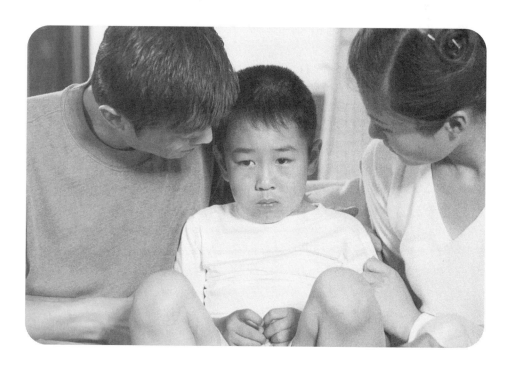

MELISSA'S STORY PART 3

10. During the next weeks and months, what did Melissa's father do to support her?

11. What did Melissa's mother do to support her?

12. What did Frank and Melissa do together?

13. How did Justin react? In other words, what did he say?

EXERCISE 4: Understand Types of Offers

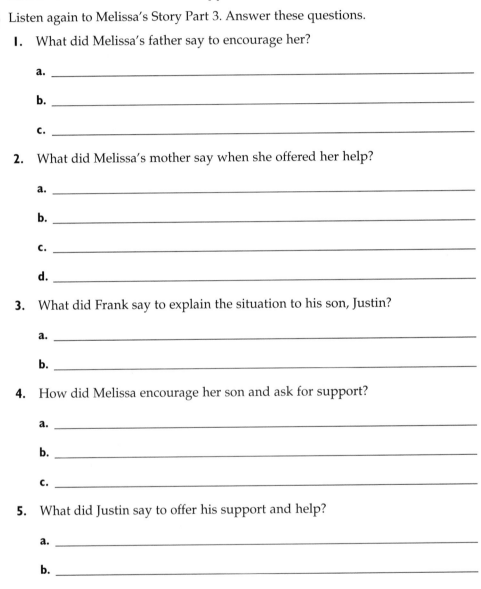 Listen again to Melissa's Story Part 3. Answer these questions.

1. What did Melissa's father say to encourage her?

   a. _____

   b. _____

   c. _____

2. What did Melissa's mother say when she offered her help?

   a. _____

   b. _____

   c. _____

   d. _____

3. What did Frank say to explain the situation to his son, Justin?

   a. _____

   b. _____

4. How did Melissa encourage her son and ask for support?

   a. _____

   b. _____

   c. _____

5. What did Justin say to offer his support and help?

   a. _____

   b. _____

   c. _____

STEP 3: Speaking

CULTURAL POINT

More Talk about Serious News

When people discuss sad news, it is important to be helpful and to not hurt others' feelings.

In the United States, there are some appropriate ways to act. There are also some comments to say that can help the situation.

Share Sad News

- Prepare, and practice what you want to say in advance.
- Be clear, direct, and specific.
- Sound serious.
- Don't avoid telling the news.
- Plan to stay calm if others become emotional.

Respond to Sad News

- Make sure you understand the details. Don't just guess and imagine.
- Ask factual questions.
- Try not to become too emotional.
- Say an encouraging comment to the person who told the news.

EXERCISE 5: Listen for Details I

 A. Listen to "A Serious Discussion 1." Answer the questions.

B. Work with a partner. Role play this conversation. Notice the intonation and emotion.

C. Share with your class.

1. Did the brother carefully prepare what he wanted to say?

2. Did the brother ask for any specific help?

3. How did his sister react?

4. Did the brother know specific information about the cost of getting help?

5. Did the sister say anything to encourage her brother?

EXERCISE 6: Listen for Details 2

 A. Listen to "A Serious Discussion 2." Answer the questions.

1. What specific help did the brother ask for?

2. What specific information did the brother give about insurance?

3. How did the sister react?

4. In the end, what kind of help did the sister offer?

5. Is this discussion more useful than the first one? Why?

B. Work with a partner. Role play this conversation. Notice the intonation and emotion.

C. Create a similar conversation. Write it and practice.

D. Share with your class.

ANALYSIS

EXERCISE 7: **Decide on Appropriateness**

Discuss these comments with your classmates. Decide if they are appropriate or inappropriate ways to react to serious news. (Hint: There are four comments of each type.)

Comments	Appropriate	Inappropriate
1. That's really boring. Don't you have any exciting news?		
2. Oh, that's awful news! What can I do to help you?		
3. Those doctors are really stupid. You don't look sick.		
4. I'm really sorry to tell you this, but I can't do this alone. I need your help.		
5. Look, I have cancer, so you need to start helping out around here.		
6. I don't believe it. You're lying! Your test results must be wrong.		
7. Doctor, are you sure? I am really surprised. I had no idea that my problems were so serious. What can I do now?		
8. No matter what happens, I will always be here to help you.		

EXERCISE 8: **Categorize Responses**

 Listen to the recording and check (✓) the boxes to show if the speakers are *complaining, sympathetic, encouraging,* or *neutral.* (Hint: See Chapter 14 for a review of these expressions.)

	Complaining	Sympathetic	Encouraging	Neutral
1.		✓		
2.				
3.				
4.				
5.				
6.				
7.				
8.				

EXERCISE 9: Express Sympathy, Encouragement, and Help

Imagine that you are in these situations. What would you say? Write your answers and share them with your classmates.

1. How can you encourage an older person who has a serious health problem?

2. If you were talking with a friend who has cancer (or another serious illness), what would you say?

3. Imagine that your boyfriend or girlfriend (or your husband or wife) became very ill. What would you do to show support?

 *Online Study Center*   **Improve Your Grade**

STEP 4: Stepping It Up

EXERCISE 10: Tell a Story

Discuss with a partner. Partners should respond with comments of sympathy. Then, change partners and discuss the same questions again.

1. Have you ever been very sick? Tell the story of your illness.

2. Have you known someone with cancer (or another serious illness)? Can you tell their story?

EXERCISE 11: Listen and Understand Others

Choose one of the following activities to practice the skills you have learned. Share your experiences in class.

1. Individually, find someone who is a cancer survivor and who speaks English. Ask if you can visit with the person. Listen to that person's story about how cancer has affected his or her life. Provide encouragement and sympathy.

2. Join a fund-raising activity in your area that is connected to a serious illness. Raise money by walking and getting pledges (promises of money) from friends and family. During the walk, find a chance to talk with an illness survivor. Listen to that person talk about his or her story. Provide encouragement and sympathy.

EXERCISE 12: **Prepare the Project**

Return to the groups that you formed in Chapter 14, Exercise 15. Make a list of interview questions in your group. Type or write them clearly on a piece of paper and ask your instructor for approval. At the end of this unit, there are more guidelines for the project. The following questions can help with your interview planning.

1. What would you like to ask a senior citizen in your community?

2. What kinds of stories could seniors tell (e.g., the most romantic moment, the best family times, the most exciting adventure)?

3. What activities do seniors usually do after they retire?

EXERCISE 13: **Evaluate Your Learning**

Check the goals that you achieved in English.

☐ 1. Listen and understand a long story.

☐ 2. Tell a story.

☐ 3. Distinguish appropriate and inappropriate comments.

☐ 4. Listen to and respond to serious news.

☐ 5. Express sympathy, encouragement, and offers to help.

 *Online Study Center*   **ACE the Test!**

 *Online Teaching Center*   **Unit Assessment**

Instructors: Print out the unit assessment. Play the appropriate assessment recording for the class.

PROJECT

Interact with Senior Citizens

SYNTHESIS

Goal

You will listen to complaints, provide encouragement, express sympathy, and listen to a long story.

Description

You will interview senior citizens outside of class. There may be a senior center in the community where your class can go. However, if one is not available, each pair or group will find a retired senior citizen in the community to interview.

Preparation 1: Choose Your Senior Citizens

See Chapter 14, Exercise 15.

Preparation 2: Make Interview Questions

See Chapter 15, Exercise 12.

Interview

Your instructor will talk to you about arranging a time for the interview. You will use your interview questions to talk and listen to the seniors. You should take turns asking questions. All students should take notes. Decide with your instructor about taking pictures, showing items, or sharing food from your native country.

Presentation

In class, your groups should share their experiences and summarize their conversations. This may mean a poster exhibit, a short oral presentation, or an informal discussion.

Feedback

Evaluate your abilities to do the goals for the project. Discuss the following questions:

1. How did you do on your project?
2. Did you participate in all of the steps of this project?
3. During the interview:
   Did you hear complaints?
   Did you offer sympathy or encouragement?
   Were you able to listen to a long story and understand some of the details?
4. What was useful about the experience of talking with senior citizens?
5. Are there any suggestions for future classes?

Assessment Chart

Your instructor will use this scoring guide to assess your work throughout the project.

Project Assessment Chart

Group Members					
Criteria	0 None of the Time	2 Some of the Time	3 Most of the Time	4 All of the Time	Comments
1. Research Did each student hand in a list of possible senior centers or people?					
2. Make Interview Questions Did each group turn in interview questions for approval? Were their questions appropriate?					
3. Interview Did each student ask at least one question? Did they show sympathy or encouragement?					
4. Present Did the report include all of the necessary information? Was the presentation creative and interesting?					
Total Points:					

APPENDIX

Chapter 3, Exercise 7: Persuade Others in Monologues

Cut the strips into individual game pieces. Each group uses one set of all the Compliments, Needs, and Requests. In small groups, spread out the cut-up pieces and divide them into three groups, with all Compliments together, all Needs together, and all Requests together. Then match each Compliment with a Need and a Request to create monologues.

Compliments

You are really good with computers.
You are so good with sociology.
I heard that you know all about using the Internet.
I think that you are good at shopping. You really know where to buy the latest fashions.
You are really good with tools, like hammers and nails.
You are so good at writing reports.
I heard that you know all about mathematics.
I think that you are good at saving money.
You are really strong. Look at those muscles.
You are so good at cleaning things.

Needs

I really need to learn how to e-mail my friend.
I could really use your help with my sociology homework.
I need to find out how to buy a book online.
I have a big job interview coming up, but I don't know what to wear.
I need to hang a big picture on the wall.
I could really use your help with writing my English report.
I need to do loads of math homework.
I really need to get my school budget ready for my folks.
I rented a moving truck because I am moving this weekend.
I could really use your help to clean my new apartment before I move in.

Requests

Can you help me?
Could you help me?
Could you give me some suggestions?
Could you take some time to help me?
Can you come over to my place and help me hang the picture?
Do you have a few minutes later today to help me?
Do you have some time to help me with my homework?
Could you help me check over my budget?
Could you help me move my stuff to my new apartment?
Do you have some time on Friday to help me clean?

APPENDIX

UNIT II: Buying a Computer

Chapter 4, Exercise 14: Show Your Knowledge

Cut the strips into individual game pieces. Each group uses one complete set. Turn the pieces facedown on a desk and divide them among all group members. Take turns drawing pictures of the vocabulary. Other members guess what the student artist is drawing.

monitor	mouse
CD-Rom drive	floppy disk
keyboard	mouse pad
printer	computer screen
headphones	software
surfing (or searching) the Internet	typing homework
playing computer games	sending e-mail
listening to music	making digital video movies

3

APPENDIX

Chapter 6, Exercise 10, and Unit 2 Project:
Make a Computer Store

Before you open your store, fill in a separate receipt for each item that you plan to sell with the price of that item. Attach the receipts to the pictures of the items so that your customers can see the prices. When someone buys an item, give half of the receipt to the customer and keep the other half for yourself.

Store Name: _____

Item

_____

Selling Price

$ _____.00

✂ CUT OR TEAR HERE

Store Name: _____

STORE KEEPS THIS PART ▼

Item _____

Sold for $_____.00

APPENDIX

UNIT II: Buying a Computer

Unit 2 Project: Make a Computer Store Inventory

At the end of the sale, calculate the results for each group on a copy of the Store Inventory form.

Store Inventory

Store Name: _____

Opening Date: _____

Number of items for sale = _____

Cash Register Amount = $ _____.00

+ _____

+ _____

Closing Date: _____

Number of items not sold = _____

Cash Register Amount = $ _____.00

Store Owners:

1. _____

2. _____

3. _____

4. _____

CREDITS

Text Credits

p. 68–69 Jeffrey Parker, Ph.D., "Some Speculations on the Social Skills Basis of Friendship Formation and Maintenance" excerpted from Asher, S. R., Parker, J. G., & Walker, D. (1996): "Distinguishing friendship from acceptance: Implications for intervention and assessment." In W. M. Bukowski, A. F. Newcomb, & W. W. Hartup (Eds.), *The Company They Keep: Friendships in childhood and adolescence* (pp. 366–405). Cambridge University Press.

p. 124 www.cancer.gov/cancertopics/factsheet/Sites-Types/general; Cancer: Questions and Answers. http://www.cancer.gov./cancertopics/When-Someone-You-Love-Is-Treated/page2; Who is a caregiver?

Photo Credits

p. 1   © Chuck Savage/Corbis
p. 8   © Tom Grill/Corbis
p. 9   © Roy Morsch/Corbis
p. 11   © Grace/zefa/Corbis
p. 14   © Darius Ramazani/zefa/Corbis
p. 19   © Poppy Berry/zefa/Corbis
p. 23   © George Shelley/Corbis
p. 32   © Royalty-Free/Corbis
p. 35   © Leland Bobbé/Corbis
p. 39   *left:* © G. Schuster/zefa/Corbis
        right: © Royalty-Free/Corbis
p. 40   *left:* © Adrianna Williams/zefa/Corbis
        right: © Chris Collins/Corbis
p. 49   Ryan McVay/Getty Images, Inc.
p. 56   Mary Kate Denny/PhotoEdit
p. 65   © Tom Stewart/Corbis
p. 69   Michael Newman/PhotoEdit

p. 70   © Royalty-Free/Corbis
p. 77   © Royalty-Free/Corbis
p. 88   Larry Wright, Cagle Cartoons
p. 93   © Tom & Dee Ann McCarthy/Corbis
p. 101 Barros & Barros/Getty Images, Inc.
p. 109 Stephen Derr/Getty Images, Inc.
p. 113 © Jim Craigmyle/Corbis
p. 114 © Jim Craigmyle/Corbis
p. 121 Sean Justice/Getty Images, Inc.
p. 124 *left:* Kent Wood/Peter Arnold, Inc.
        right: Ed Reschke/Peter Arnold, Inc.
p. 125 Photodisc/Getty Images, Inc.
p. 133 © Royalty-Free/Corbis
p. 138 Photodisc/Getty Images, Inc.
p. 143 © Yang Liu/Corbis
p. 146 Amy Etra/PhotoEdit
p. 148 © Gene Blevins/Corbis

Unit 4 Assessment

(1) http://www.marthastewart.com/page.jhtml?type=learn-cat&id=cat20242; About the Show: Martha Stewart Bio
(2) http://www.blinkbits.com/bits/viewtopic/martha_stewart_to_contest_sec_insider_trading_charges.?t=9437346; Martha Stewart to contest SEC insider trading charges; AP
(3) http://www.realitytv.about.com/od/theapprenticemartha/ss/MarthaTrivia.htm; All About Martha Stewart; Latoya West

(4) http://manhattan.about.com/od/citylife1/p/marthastewart.htm; Martha Stewart Biography; Pamela Skillings
(5) http://en.wikipedia.org/wiki/Martha_Stewart; Martha Stewart; Wikipedia
(6) http://tlc.discovery.com/fansites/martha/about/about.html; About Martha Stewart